The Internet Public Library Handbook

By Joseph Janes, David Carter,
Annette Lagace, Michael McLennen,
Sara Ryan, and Schelle Simcox

NEAL-SCHUMAN NETGUIDE SERIES

NEAL-SCHUMAN PUBLISHERS, INC.
NEW YORK   LONDON

Published by Neal-Schuman Publishers, Inc.
100 Varick Street
New York, NY 10013

Library of Congress Cataloging-in-Publication Data

The Internet public library handbook / Joseph Janes . . . [et al.].
        p.   cm.   -- (Neal-Schuman NetGuide series)
    Includes index.
    ISBN 1–55570–344–5
    1. Internet Public Library.   2. Digital libraries—United States.
  I. Janes, Joseph.   II. Series: Neal-Schuman net-guide series.
    ZA4082.U63   I555 1999
    025'.00285 -- dc21
                                                            98–48983
                                                              CIP

Contents

List of Figures

Preface

The Internet Public Library Handbook is not just for librarians! Although our perspective comes directly from our training and experience in libraries, and we can speak most directly to our colleagues in the library/information world, we also draw heavily on our experiences in computer science, telecommunications, design, and other relevant fields. This blend of expertise and knowledge has served us well, and (we think) can be a model for others.

We've written this book with two particular audiences in mind: librarians *and* anyone else who builds or maintains information resources, especially via the Internet. Of course, there's a significant overlap between these groups. Our intent is to help information providers:

- plan, build, and maintain collections of Web-based resources;
- consider, develop, and design services to meet their users' special needs;
- design and plan original, "natively" Web-based information resources;
- develop services to answer reference inquiries via e-mail; and
- think critically about issues of funding and support of network-based information services.

THE INTERNET PUBLIC LIBRARY

The Internet Public Library (IPL) is the Internet's first and only "public library." Our site (www.ipl.org) comprises the world's largest collection of online texts, newspapers, serial publications, and general reference resources. Our reference service was the first general-purpose reference service on the Net. Our staff has answered more than ten thousand questions. IPL staff and associates have developed original, award-winning exhibitions; reference resources; and children's stories.

We believe librarians have much to contribute to the development of our virtual world. Our "public library" has been visited by users from over 130 countries. We presently average over 20,000 users per day, an average of 1 every 4 seconds, 24 hours a day.

Those of us who have been part of the Internet Public Library (IPL) since its opening in 1995 have had the extraordinary privilege of being able to think about what librarianship means in an increasingly networked, digital world. Moreover, we've explored our ideas and experimented—actually building things and offering services—all in the context of a public library for the community of people who live on the Internet.

With that privilege, however, comes an obligation to share both our successes and our (painfully learned) lessons with our colleagues in the library and information professions and the broader networked world. We've had some notable successes and projects we're very proud of, and more than a few things that just didn't work or that we weren't able to do for lack of resources, time, expertise, or the right idea. Our intent in writing *The Internet Public Library Handbook* is to convey what the IPL has done and what can best be described as the IPL "experience": how we view the world, the approach we take to our work, and the ideas and values that guide what we do. We hope librarians can then use our experiences to help them avoid "reinventing the wheel" and can use our experiences to make their virtual libraries more successful.

ORGANIZATION AND CONTENTS

Chapter 1 presents a vision for where librarianship might—and should—head in the emerging information environment. Chapter 1 also includes a brief outline of the origins and history of the Internet Public Library project, including the decisions that influenced its development and the ideas that gave it form.

Following this broad overview, we discuss the particulars. Chapter 2 covers the assembly and maintenance of collections of networked resources. Specific aspects covered in Chapter 2 include scanning and searching for materials, organization and subject access decisions, database construction, locating resources, evaluation, serving the outside world, and ongoing maintenance. A vision for the future of Internet collection development is also presented.

Chapter 3 outlines the steps involved in building new resources for the Web and in adapting existing content to this medium. The major steps outlined include understanding users, identifying and addressing design issues, working in teams, thinking about access concerns, and dealing with technical support and maintenance. This chapter illustrates the issues and decisions by highlighting two IPL projects: POTUS (Presidents of the United States), one of our original reference resources, and the Exhibit Hall, our showcase for design and nontextual content.

Chapter 4 looks at providing services for young people. It discusses why we do it, what is appropriate, what kids are like these days, IPL-specific ideas and projects (including the Youth and Teen divisions), and feedback and maintenance; it concludes with ideas about what other libraries can do.

Chapter 5 deals with reference. Specifically, it emphasizes the IPL's e-mail-based Ask a Question reference service, including the motivation for this service, why it's important, technical aspects, and the process we've refined (including the virtual reference interview). Chapter 5 also considers issues of staffing and scale, as well as characteristics of "physical" reference that need to be attended to in a virtual environment.

Chapter 6 covers money and its importance in the virtual library's environment. Since public libraries are "free" (unless you're trying to run one), no funding base exists for a networked-based community service, and there is as yet a resistance to paying for information via the Internet. Issues of revenue generation have been important for the IPL and, we think, for other libraries as we move together into this new environment.

From the beginning, the IPL has been motivated by a desire to see what the practice of librarianship had to offer the networked world, and what the power and interconnections of the networks meant for librarianship. What follows is our work—so far—in figuring this out and the lessons we've learned. We hope that it will help you in your quest to provide information services on the Web.

Chapter 1

Adapting to the New Information Environment

Joseph Janes with Michael McLennen

SO WHAT'S A LIBRARIAN TO DO?

More people logged on to the Internet last year than set foot in any public library. The total amount of information kept in digital form will very shortly exceed the amount stored on paper, and soon after that will exceed the sum total of all forms of hard copy combined. A serious proposal was made to the Texas state board of education that schoolchildren be issued computers next year instead of new textbooks. And we could tell you hundreds of similar facts and stories. Your reaction to such developments may range from "How scary!" to "It's about time!"—but in any case, we are all being swept along in the wake of the march of information technology.

So what does this book have to do with any of that? Many of you (we hope) have heard of the Internet Public Library. Some of you have used it directly, others have demonstrated it in classrooms or used us as a referral service for difficult or Internet-related reference questions. Even if you have never heard of us before, you may have been intrigued by our name—what goes on in the strange realm where "Internet" meets "public library"?

It was partly to answer this last question that the Internet Public Library was founded. In the years since then, we have created a highly successful place for people to go on the Net when they want to find freely available, high-quality information. But much more than that, we have learned how to take these two worlds and make each one support the other. On one hand, we have learned a lot about how to apply the time-tested principles of librarianship to the decentralized, unmediated world of the Internet. On the other hand, we have figured out how to use the newly available technology in the most efficient way to learn about librarianship. If either notion intrigues you, then this book is for you.

In the process of undertaking this mind-boggling project, we've learned some important lessons about collection building and maintenance, organization of networked resources, reference service, building original resources, working with and for young people, getting money (and dealing with the lack thereof)—precisely the sorts of issues facing libraries of all types regardless of environment or community. Part of the reason we undertook the IPL in the first place was to share the lessons we learned with our professional colleagues.

We have gone in many different directions, some more productive than others but all enlightening. Among the individual projects we have undertaken are the following:

- We started and now maintain the first "public library" of and for the Internet world.
- We have amassed the world's largest collections of online texts, newspapers, serial publications, and general reference resources.
- Our reference service, the first general-purpose reference service on the Net, has answered more than 10,000 questions to date.
- We have developed new curricula for librarians in training, part of the course of study at the School of Information at the University of Michigan, which hosts the IPL.
- Working under our auspices, our staff members and associates have developed original and award-winning exhibitions, reference resources, and children's stories.

All of these accomplishments pale in comparison to what can be done, and is being done, by the library community in public libraries, schools, and companies around the world. We hope that the lessons we have learned and the models we have developed will be of help to you in developing your own services, resources, and curricula. If this is the case, then the effort we have put into this book (and the project as a whole) will have been well worth it. The biggest lesson we have learned during this project is that no matter how the world of information changes, skilled librarians are more necessary than ever.

In the rest of this chapter, I try to amplify these notions. First, I share some ideas about trends in the overall "information environment" in which we live and work, followed by some ideas about what the library profession can do to react to these trends and to some degree shape them. The chapter also includes a brief history of the IPL project, discussing our motivations and some of the early decisions we made, and finishes with a brief overview of the rest of the book.

THE EMERGING INFORMATION ENVIRONMENT

It will come as no surprise to anybody reading this book that the world of information is changing. In fact, we can all reel off a long list of technological developments (writing, paper, printing, cataloging, photography, sound recording, microforms, computers) that have completely transformed the information professions. The catch is that the pace of technological change is constantly accelerating. For a profession whose business it is to keep abreast of the latest in available information and the latest needs of customers—and to link the two of them—there are days when it appears that there's no way to keep up with long-term trends and still attend to the day-to-day requirements of the job. If you're feeling that way, it may come as some small consolation to know that you're probably right, and you certainly aren't alone.

More, Faster, Bigger

For several years now, computer industry analysts have been quoting something known as "Moore's Law"—an observation that, over time, the processing speed and memory capacity of the computer equipment you can buy for a given amount of money has roughly doubled every 18 months. From our perspective, this phenomenon is the cause of the frustrating effect that computer equipment becomes obsolete almost immediately after we buy it. On the other hand, it has also produced a continuous expansion of what computers are capable of doing for us. Enormous databases that would have been unmanageable ten years ago are now served out contentedly by that machine on the corner of your desk, while your Web browser regularly churns through computations that would have swamped your old 386 PC just in the course of laying out the graphics-heavy pages it displays for you.

This trend shows no sign of slowing down. In fact, it is constantly accelerating at an exponential rate. In terms of raw computing power we may well be approaching a point where computers are getting more capable at a rate faster than we can imagine more complicated things for them to do. This is, in other words, a point where we can just about take computing power for granted. If you want to build or design some computer application that requires monstrous amounts of computer power or memory or bandwidth, you just have to wait a bit and it will be available soon.

Another aspect of technology that is growing in a similar manner is the degree of interconnection between and among computers, information sources, and people. In this realm, by contrast, we have definitely *not* reached a "taken-for-granted" point. In fact, nobody can really be sure what kinds of things will be possible when the degree of interconnection has doubled, say, ten times over (for a multiplication factor of more than 1,000). It is simply beyond our comprehension. And yet, we will reach this point sometime in the next 10 to 15 years if present trends continue. It is easy to extrapolate that the people who will be at the forefront of the information professions in 10 to 15 years are those who can exercise their imaginations to the fullest and determine how best to use this newfound interconnectedness.

The Shift in Publishing

For most of human history, it has been hard to get published. When it costs a lot of money to have a printing press or publishing company—when you have to invest in machines, staff, editors, advertising, shipping, paper, and all the rest of it—it becomes a nontrivial matter to set up shop and become a publisher. To be sure, people could (and did) self-publish, but the potential audience was quite small indeed, usually limited to friends or people who were willing to buy or even take free copies of whatever was offered, which they might well look on somewhat dubiously because it wasn't professional looking.

The technological trends listed above are changing all that. The investment needed to produce some sort of document and make it available to a global audience is now quite small. All one needs is a computer to create it and somewhere to put it. Add access to technology provided by many public libraries and free Web site hosts like Geocities, and the costs drop to zero. Getting "published" (using that word somewhat loosely) is now considerably easier.

This means that the kinds of controls we were used to in the world of information are loosening. Specifically there are two kinds of control: editorial and intellectual. Editorial control helps the reader by checking facts, making the writing easier to read, and providing an imprimatur of quality. If Bennett Cerf published something at Random House, one knew it was probably worth reading. Intellectual control (cataloging, indexing, and so on) is provided by librarians, and allows retrieval based on content and other characteristics. When the flow of information items is from a manageable number of known and trusted sources, the kinds of organizational structures we've developed over the decades not only make sense but are necessary.

That is all changing. Editorial controls and oversight are no longer required before information items see the light of day and reach a very wide potential audience, and when those items can come from literally anywhere, there are no good mechanisms to provide the sort of intellectual control we've grown accustomed to.

Furthermore, these items are less stable than their more traditional counterparts. When a document lives solely in digital format, it can be continually changed. With some documents, such as stock reports or weather forecasts, this is a great advantage. How, though, do we handle documents that need never reach a "final" form? How are they to be cited? How do you know which version is the most recent or "correct" one?

In this fluid environment incredible creativity and innovation are now possible. New forms, genres, and kinds of resources will emerge as a result of these technological and publishing trends. Early examples include the Internet Movie Database (us.imdb. com) and Presidents of the United States (www.ipl.org/ref/ POTUS).

Finally, without tight editorial controls there is and will be just much more stuff out there. With the bottlenecks and hurdles of traditional publishing gone, there is nothing to stem the tide of stuff from overrunning us all. It remains to be seen what sort of economic model will be established; advertising alone is not yet able to support the Internet as is, but no doubt the creativity of the marketplace will figure out some way to make it all work. That doesn't mean that such models will be felicitous or even pleasant, but it's likely they'll arise.

The Legacy of Print

An increasing amount of information items are "born digital"— created using word processing, digital imaging, or sound recording. Some of these items make their way to analog media such as paper, but their "master" versions are digital; hence they open the way for digital approaches for long-term storage, description, organization, access, and so on.

A large number of information items, however, are not now and never have been digital. Countless books and magazines and newspapers and audiocassettes and microforms are just sitting in libraries all over the world. Many if not most of those items will never be digitized, unless that technology becomes dramatically cheaper and quicker; at present it is simply too costly and time-consuming to contemplate a massive conversion process. In addition, as long as this material stays in print, copyright owners will perceive a lower threat of infringement, and many users will see the material as less attractive because it may be less immediately available.

Therefore, all this new information, both digital and analog, is being added to the large repositories of traditional media. These different media require different storage mechanisms and procedures, different ways of purchasing and acquiring them, different ways of organizing and making them available, different ways of educating users and staff, different modes of use, different intellectual property concerns—and the list goes on.

For now and for the foreseeable future, librarians will be simultaneously working in the library of yesterday, the library of today, and the library of tomorrow.

People Don't Care

Finally, for most people, the process of looking for information items is less important than the result. To be sure, there are people who are highly engaged by the process of information seeking and love the thrill of the hunt. Many of them become librarians, and we may often believe that everybody else is (or should be) as interested in the process as we are. That is not to say that we should abandon the educational mission of librarianship, but rather that we should keep in mind that getting an answer or a book or the right magazine articles or just some help and understanding may be what people are really after.

As an aside, it's interesting to wonder whether people will care more about the process as they live more in an information-based environment. As more people spend more time using networked information, and try to find things on a more regular basis, it may well be that the process becomes more important and therefore more engaging to them. The rise of Web sites such as Search Engine Watch (www.searchenginewatch.com), which provides information and even gossip about search engines for a mass audience, would have been unthinkable even a few years ago. Perhaps people will care more as they gain experience. One wonders to what extent this will be a net benefit for information professionals.

IMPACT ON LIBRARIANSHIP

We live in a very fast-changing world, and the state of information is one of its most rapidly changing aspects. A profession such as ours, which depends on and is an integral part of the state of information, must therefore be profoundly affected by such rapid changes.

We are facing a complex and challenging situation. The basic technologies that enable us to do our work are growing in power and speed at an exponential pace. The number and variety of people who are publishing their ideas and words are similarly rapidly expanding. New kinds of resources are on the horizon, and the ones we thought we knew are becoming less stable and reliable. The sheer volume of potentially interesting information staggers the imagination. Editorial and intellectual controls are ebbing. At the same time, there's a lot of print out there that isn't going to become digital any time soon, and to top it all off, most people don't care how they find material so long as it gets found.

In the past, we in the information business had to contend with two scarce commodities: money and content. We have almost always had limited resources with which to acquire and process materials and to make them available—hence the rise of such services as interlibrary loan and shared cataloging. (If libraries were better funded, would OCLC ever have arisen?) And even then, there were just so many things to buy. Granted, traditional book and serial publishing has produced an ever-growing amount of information, but editorial processes and economic realities meant that only just so many things could get published.

This situation is about to change. Perhaps the most profound outcome of the technology "explosion" is that, although money will still be a limiting factor for us, the scarcity of information won't be. Information won't be scarce, it will be plentiful. This may seem like a real boon, and in many ways it is. When publishing is easy, those small and marginal points of view will be much easier to get at, and topics that interest only a very few people can be made available.

But so far, we as a profession are unprepared for this world. Much of our professional practice developed over the last couple of hundred years is based on the scarcity of information. When information is plentiful, we try to apply familiar concepts (for example, assigning Library of Congress Subject Headings to Web sites and creating MARC records for them), but these approaches will often be doomed to fail because they simply aren't appropriate. Book catalogs and journal indexes made sense for those kinds of items in their technological and economic contexts. All bets are off, though, and new approaches will have to be developed to deal with the new environment.

So money will be scarce and information plentiful. The other scarce commodity with which we will have to contend is more esoteric but equally important: human attention. In a world where technology fosters a round-the-clock global audience for billions of information items of all kinds, there are only so many things any one person can focus on. People have been complaining about information overload for many years—and that was before the Internet.

As attention becomes more precious, it will have to be allocated more carefully. People will have to make more difficult decisions about what to attend to, and they will need guidance to make those decisions easier. What programs will they watch on television? What movies will they go see? What Web sites will they surf? Which search engine or directory will they use to find information on the Net? Quick and easy guidance (remember, the process is less important than the outcome) will become increasingly prized and valued. This guidance will come, as it usually does, from convenient sources: friends, colleagues, as well as trusted sources like newspapers and critics. Will libraries and librarians be on that list?

HOW LIBRARIANSHIP SHOULD REACT

Librarianship must evolve and adapt to this new information environment. Librarians are remarkably good at this sort of thing: we have repeatedly developed new mechanisms for identifying good resources, assembling collections, describing and organizing items for access, helping people use those collections and find things, and preserving the human record for future generations. Each new technological challenge has been met and new practices and services developed to further our work. And now we must do it again.

We must develop new techniques, strategies, and services to support intellectual activity and communication. As the way in which knowledge is represented changes, so must the way it is organized and accessed. Moreover, the way that knowledge is created will change, as new generations of scholars and artists and creators take advantage of the capabilities of emerging technologies.

The life cycle of knowledge—creation, recording, collection, description, organization, retrieval, access, evaluation, use, and then feeding back into creation—will be profoundly changed and will reflect the trends we discussed above. Our sector of that cycle will not only change but broaden, as libraries and librarians become more involved in the creation of new knowledge and guides to new knowledge. At the same time, the publishing world will become more involved with organization and access issues as publishers begin to interact more directly with users and become concerned with making their products easy to use and find.

The techniques and services we develop must reflect the technological and economic world in which we live. They also must be convenient and easy to use. If people are more interested in the result than the process, then the process must be transparent or at least minimal, or people will rarely take time (ever more precious) to learn or use the tools. Services must also speak directly to individuals by being personalizable and customizable. Services such as My Yahoo and customizable news sites on the Web are only the beginning of the drive toward mass individualization via the networks. So far, people have generally not been willing to spend large amounts of time and effort on customization; it is an open question whether this will change as time becomes ever more precious.

This scenario may sound like an overwhelming challenge for an already overburdened and undersupported profession, and it is indeed a daunting prospect. The prize, though, is that this new information world will enable librarians to do what they have always wanted to do, but couldn't. Librarianship, at its core, is about getting items of information out of one person's head and into somebody else's. For the last several thousand years, that process has been difficult. Now, however, the potential exists not only to make those information items vastly more plentiful and cheap, but also to make direct connections between people in a highly interconnected world. There will still be financial and retrieval problems (in fact, retrieval will become increasingly difficult unless and until we figure out how to improve it), but the potential is there for boundless sharing of ideas, thoughts, knowledge, and stories.

So how do we do all this? It will not be easy, but it may be straightforward. We must do what we have always done; we must learn and understand and use the tools and technologies at hand to do what we all know libraries and librarians do:

- Be an expression of the communities we serve—schools, colleges, cities, businesses, organizations, governments, and so on.

- Try to improve, enlighten and educate those communities.
- Be concerned with users and their needs, and the uses of information knowledge.
- Describe, organize, and provide intellectual control for information items so that they may be retrieved and used.
- Preserve and conserve the human record for generations to come.
- Support and fight for such values as intellectual freedom, equality of access, and literacy.
- Participate in the deeply human need to share our stories and learn from each other.

This last item is probably the most critical, because it underlies all the others. We as a species have been telling our stories to each other since we developed language skills. We developed writing and art and drama and science to feed that hunger to know ourselves and our world and each other. Librarianship is the profession that helps those stories to be told and heard. A discussion in one of the early IPL seminars came to the conclusion that literacy was the glue that held societies together— that we recorded what made us who we are so that new generations could read and understand and participate. Without the ability to take in those stories, people are less connected. Librarians make those bonds stronger.

But how can we possibly surmount this exploding world of information coming at us from all sides? "Indexing the Internet" hasn't worked, and there just aren't enough of us to do everything that would need to be done. If we were to increase the number of librarians by an order of magnitude and turn them loose on the Web to index it or catalog it, it might start to make a difference, but that's not a happy prospect.

To be sure, each of us can do something. Lots of libraries have installed computers with Internet connections for free public access, taught classes and developed instructional materials for patrons, and built Web sites for their communities' specific needs. These are all great ideas and good beginnings.

Viral Librarianship

If we really want to have an impact, though, if we really want to make a difference and make librarianship a powerful and vibrant force in the new information world, we need to think bigger. We need to make what librarianship is and does much more widely understood and respected and followed as a model for the networked world. That does not mean simply sharing the good word of MARC records and waiting for the Internet to adopt them, because that won't happen.

It does mean that we must think of librarianship as a virus (a beneficial one, to be sure)—a way of infecting the information world with our perspectives, ideals, values, and techniques. If we can propagate what we do and how we do it, we could become part of the very fabric of the information world and thus have much broader impact than we have simply on our own.

To achieve this, we must work well, cooperatively, often, visibly, and "cool."

- We must work *well*—that goes without saying!
- We must take advantage of the available technology to work *cooperatively*, as we already do so well. Given the major impact of OCLC, imagine what the connectivity of the Internet could mean for, say, cooperative or specialized reference services, collection building, continuing education, and sharing of best practices.
- We must work *often*, because the more examples and the larger base of experience and cooperation we have the more we can offer each other and the world.
- It is very important that we work *visibly*. We must be in our communities and out on the Net, and be aggressive and loud about what we do and why. Nobody on the Net gets noticed by good works and clean living alone.
- *Cool* is the great commodity of the Net, at least so far. Cool will get you a long way, and when it's backed up by great work it will get you even farther. We need to attract cool people to the profession and smash the old professional stereotype wherever possible.

A word on communities. When we use that word, we are usually referring to groups of people who live in the same area or who share some characteristic. It's an overused word, and it probably doesn't make sense to talk about "the Internet community" because it really doesn't exist—it's simply a bunch of shared telecommunications protocols bringing together the millions of people worldwide on the Internet. But the Internet will surely foster the development of many smaller communities, based on mutual affinity and interest. Such groups have already existed, but now they can form around almost anything, and the global reach and rich interconnectivity of the Internet means they can form around very small or esoteric interests.

These groups—current listservs, Usenet groups, chat rooms, Web rings, and so on—are only the first instances; they could become much more important as the Net becomes a more prominent aspect of daily life. If people spend a lot of time in those "virtual communities," these "communities" might even become more important than their geographic communities.

If we look at what local communities do, we see that they often combine resources to provide mutual services such as recreation facilities, schools, police—and libraries. The opportunity here is palpable. These new communities will require the same sorts of services that we typically think of libraries as providing: building collections of information to meet the group's need, answering questions, suggesting how to find new things and what might be good, and so on. Why not have those kinds of services, supported by these groups in Cyberspace, and staffed by librarians or at least people who follow our patterns and share our ideals? If we can infect this environment with librarianship, we can make a profound difference in the way these groups function and flourish.

WHAT YOU COULD DO: SOME IDEAS

The rest of this book gives you some concrete ideas and suggestions, based on the work of the Internet Public Library over the last few years. To finish this chapter, though, I'd like to offer a few thoughts of my own, based on the previous discussion, of what libraries might do in this new world.

Academic librarians face challenges based on the changing nature of scholarship and the communication of scholarship. The changes in the information world are already reflected in new kinds of products of scholarship which call into question whether monographs and journals will continue in their present form. These are the fundamental building blocks of academic library collections, and as they change, those collections may change. In addition, publishers are continuing to explore new means of selling or licensing journals and databases.

Academic librarians thus must find ways to provide single points of access to multiple sources of information: their local catalogs, locally mounted databases, in-house products, indexing and abstracting services, and electronic journals, not to mention their print resources. In addition, they must help their users understand what all these various sources are and how to use them and the information found therein. They must build collections under nontraditional circumstances (including potentially not owning but rather renting or licensing resources by the year or per use), and those collections must take into account users not yet born and research questions not yet asked.

Perhaps a group of libraries from peer or cooperating institutions could work cooperatively on network-based reference and collection development. This idea has been around for a long time in the academic world, but it can be extended easily into the networked environment. Each library could focus on a particular subject area or set of areas, in which they already have staff or collection strength. Using networked technology, reference and research inquiries from the set of institutions could be forwarded to appropriate staff members for more detailed and comprehensive attention than one might otherwise expect. In addition, those staff members could identify and organize high-quality networked resources (including directories, databases, pathfinders, and frequently asked questions) in their subject areas. Such a service would be concerned with and identified with quality, but also with timeliness and convenience and provision of full text when available, especially when dealing with students.

Public librarians are challenged, as always, by the sheer range and variety of people they serve and the needs they bring. Public librarians must help their users understand this new information world and its benefits. Public libraries must also fight an increasing concern with inappropriate materials of all kinds on the Internet. The current debate about filtering software is not surprising, and may be only the beginning. If people fail to understand this technology and appreciate both its advantages and drawbacks, they will fail to deal rationally with it, and may perhaps decide we're better off without it. These opinions should be respected and incorporated into libraries' decisions about what to do.

Public librarians could work on mounting locally interesting or historical materials, to make them available to a wider audience. The vast majority of libraries probably have *something* interesting in their collection that somebody else on the Net wants to see. Local schools are an excellent opportunity for cooperation—taking advantage of students' enthusiasm and the school's technology, while providing a valuable learning opportunity to boot.

Public librarians are also perhaps best suited to begin the work of infusing network-based communities with librarianship. Their skills at working with local communities are a great beginning for determining how to work with and develop services for groups that form around ideas and interests. Librarians who are already part of such groups could assume those roles.

School librarians must help their students understand that these technologies are more than just bells and whistles, and they must support and participate in curricular decisions to reinforce the culture of the word. In addition to working with their colleagues in public libraries to mount local and historic resources, school librarians can help students become good publishers. This involvement goes beyond just putting up a Web page, and could include thinking about what makes information good and interesting and worthwhile, how to design it so that it's easy to use and understand, and how to find information just for fun or to support an argument or point of view. Understanding information and the processes that go into producing it will be increasingly important, and there's nothing like publishing it—and hearing from people who've read and liked it—to bring those lessons home.

OUR STORY: A BRIEF HISTORY OF THE IPL

Before my friends and colleagues tell you more about what great things they and the IPL people have done since we opened, I'd like to share a bit of history about the IPL's early days and decisions—to give you some idea about how we faced many of these same issues in building a library solely on and of the Internet.

I sometimes say that the Internet Public Library happened because I was bored. That's not strictly or entirely true. In fact, the IPL came into being as the result of a great deal of creative thought, hard work, and energy on the part of an extraordinary group of people, and its continuing presence and high quality of service are a testament to the people who have worked on it and the power of the ideas behind it.

In the fall of 1994, I was restless and perhaps a little bored. This was a time of great innovation; it was becoming increasingly clear that this thing called the Internet was going to have significant impact on libraries and librarians as on the wider world.

Sometime in September of 1994, the phrase "Internet Public Library" entered my consciousness. For several years, I had taught a seminar on the impacts of information technology, which had a different theme each time.

It occurred to me that I might use this "Internet Public Library" idea as the next theme for this course. I talked with several friends and colleagues and asked their opinion. They all said it sounded like a great idea but a lot of work. They were more correct than they knew, but I was encouraged and so went forward. I developed a prospectus for the course, which I circulated to the students in the then School of Information and Library Studies (now the School of Information) at the University of Michigan.

Here is part of that description:

> We will explore the issues involved in the merger of networking and libraries by actually planning, building, and running a public library for the Internet community. Some of the larger questions raised by such a project include:
> - To what extent do the kinds of functions traditionally seen in libraries apply to this setting?
> - To what extent do the kinds of tools and resources traditionally seen on the Internet apply to this setting?
> - What unique functions or features will be necessary or desirable in an Internet library?
>
> I would view each of those three words as equally important in conveying the intent of this project: **Internet**, **Public**, and **Library**. I think the combination of the three of them produces something quite different than any pair or individual might suggest.

From the very beginning, then, the project was motivated by one central question: *What does librarianship have to say to the network environment and vice versa?* That question proved (then and now) both provocative and attractive.

A later message to the class started with the five goals I had outlined for the class:

- finish the course more excited than when you started
- do work you and the entire group are proud of
- everybody (including me) learn a lot
- everybody (including me) have fun doing it
- everybody gets a great job at the end

This list of goals was an attempt to set the tone for the work, to help create an environment where people could explore, try things, and stretch themselves and still have fun, yet work on something that would be meaningful and real. In general, I think we succeeded on all these counts.

Our first meeting was on January 7, 1995. We met then to allow ourselves several hours in which to hash out precisely what sorts of things we wanted to do, who wanted to do what, our mission statement, and how to proceed.

Mission and Goals

The mission statement came first. After some discussion, we adopted the following:

> The mission of our Internet Public Library is to:
> * provide services and information which enhance the value of the Internet to its ever-expanding and varied community of users
> * work to broaden, diversify, and educate that community
> * communicate its creators' vision of the unique roles of library culture and traditions on the Internet

This statement conveys our collective notion of what it meant to be a "library" in this chaotic, dynamic, placeless place.

Initial Groups

After reaching consensus on the mission statement, small groups brainstormed on what exactly the IPL should be. These groups reported back and the entire class voted on what they thought were the highest priorities. The top seven were:

* Reference
* Architecture/Interfaces/Design
* Services for Librarians/Information Professionals/Schools
* Bibliographic Instruction/User Education/Information
* Literacy/Outreach/Access

- Youth Services
- Public Relations/Development/Legacy

There are some interesting omissions here. Functions that are usually labeled "technical services" in libraries were mentioned but received little support: collection development, acquisitions, serials, cataloging, description, and organization of resources. These functions were eventually established (within the rubric of Reference), but this group did not see them as high priorities at the very beginning. Other possibilities that were mentioned but did not make the list were government resources, real-time interaction with humans (later explored via the library's Mud Object Oriented or MOO), publication, art (more about this later), and a community information/bulletin board.

These groups then met to outline what they wanted to try to accomplish and how, roles within the group, and logistical matters. Several important decisions were made during those meetings and in the weeks that followed; let me highlight a few of these groups, their ideas and early work, and what that work taught us.

TECHNOLOGY

Perhaps the most important set of decisions were made around the Technology group (led by Nigel Kerr), which dealt with site architecture, design, and related issues. Their summary of that first meeting captures those decisions well:

> Goals include
> - unifying our IPL—technically, intellectually, for users; work closely with other groups
> - acquiring and managing server(s)/infrastructure
> - providing opportunities for class members to learn about architecture and technical issues (UNIX system administration, HTML, interface design, listserv moderating)
> In collaborating with other groups,
> - we want to listen to their needs,

- use that information as input to our design and decision process, and
- inform them of what we think is/is not technically possible and feasible.

In other words, this group was not going to dictate what was possible or desirable, but rather members chose to distribute themselves and act as liaisons, consultants, and advisors to the functional groups. Those groups (Reference, Youth, etc.) were told to think first about what they wanted to do, without regard for technological capability or implementation, and the Architecture group, as the Technology group was finally called, would see what could be done. This process proved vital to the success of the project—it allowed for the free flow of ideas and creativity, which then could be tempered and adjusted as necessary based on the available technology.

Getting a server was an obvious initial hurdle—when the project began, we neither had one nor knew where we might get one. We were very fortunate in this regard; Lee Liming, the school's technology administrator at the time, met with the Architecture group, heard our ideas, and volunteered to donate a spare Sparc 20 server for our use. We are still using this server (with others) to this day; without it, of course, there would not have been an IPL.

Rather than adopting technological matters as their sole province, the Architecture group saw their role as facilitating other people learning what they need and contributing as necessary. This perspective is very important in all such projects. It reinforces the central and vital notion that all information technologies are merely tools to be used. *Ideas first, tools later*.

PUBLIC RELATIONS

Then, there was the Public Relations group (led by Maria Bonn and Bradley Taylor). In early 1995 the Web was still a young and comparatively unpopulated place, but if this extraordinary work was to be seen and used, it would have to be promoted. A group of students who were interested in or had experience with public relations undertook this responsibility. The press release, sent to the world (but targeted to the library world), was extremely well written, generated great interest and enthusiasm, and raised the stakes dramatically for the work as a whole. Here is an excerpt from the text of that release:

Bold initiative heralds the creation of tomorrow's library today

The University of Michigan School of Information and Library Studies proudly announces the advent of the Internet Public Library (IPL), an innovative, on-line, 24-hour public library designed to revolutionize the way the world thinks about library services. The Internet Public Library will offer an exciting version of the library of tomorrow as envisioned by many of the brightest talents in the field today.

The response was overwhelming. So many requests for information were received (going to individuals' e-mail boxes) that we had to set up a listserv to keep people informed on the work. Subsequent messages encouraged people to subscribe to that group. The press release was sent in February; by the time the IPL opened in mid-March, over 3,000 people from around the world had subscribed.

Now, several thousand people were waiting to see what we would come up with. This was no longer a major, important class project that would be interesting, be up for a few weeks, and then be graded and become a happy memory when the class ended. It would be a real product, facing a global audience who would want to see it, use it, and perhaps even depend on it. As the number of people on the listserv grew, so did the pressure to produce a high-quality product by the deadline, at which time our child would face the world on its own.

Never underestimate the power of a well-written press release, backed up by hard work and dedication of a creative, clever group of people. *Publicity breeds accountability.*

SERVICES TO LIBRARIANS

The original mission statement committed us to share our lessons, not only with our patrons and the Internet world, but also with our professional colleagues. The Services to Librarians and Information Professionals group (led by Richard Truxall) worked on this. Their work broke into several large categories: help to librarians in getting connected to and using the Internet, examples of how libraries were using the Net, and professional resources. They wrote original documents about the Internet and how to get connected, how to use it, and how to build resources (including telnet, Web, gopher, and Veronica); they identified libraries using networks for their work; and they identified Net resources from professional organizations. They also wanted to create a calendar of meetings, conferences, and events and to foster a mentorship program to help librarians new to the network connect with more experienced colleagues.

In practice, these efforts were successful, but maintenance again became a problem, and most of the ongoing resources fell away over the years. Several people have attempted to work on this area, but we never seem to have the right idea, or the right person, or the right way of going about it. Primarily, we have not had the kind and level of contact with our colleagues that would support or foster success. *Even a strong tree needs the right soil.*

EDUCATION AND OUTREACH

Another group (led by Louise Alcorn) was very interested in issues of Education and User Outreach. These are important functions in any library, and especially in one that would almost never meet (at least in person) its users. The group's original ideas reveal their thinking—making the Internet easier to use and understand and increasing general knowledge of it and participation in it:

- to provide pathways to access points and equipment needs for potential Internet users

- to educate current and future users about techniques needed to use the Internet
- to ensure access to the IPL by a variety of users, using different platforms
- to interest non-users in the "beauty" (or "beast") of the Internet
- to solicit potential audiences as to their computing and communication needs
- to provide navigation tools to the IPL, and, through the IPL, the WWW

Much of this approach comes directly from traditional librarianship: equality and ease of access to information and resources, knowledge of those resources, and ability to use them. One aspect—navigation—was instantiated by a "building directory," an alphabetical listing of resources and areas of the IPL. The directory was available when the IPL opened, but became a maintenance problem as the library grew and expanded. The directory, though, was a precursor of similar devices common in large Web sites today, particularly the site map.

In practice, these were (and are) enormous challenges, well beyond our small capacities at the time. The IPL has always remained committed to these ideas, but has not been able to be as active as the vision of this group would have required. Much of this invaluable work goes on in libraries of all kinds, all over the country, and appropriately so. Libraries and librarians in direct contact with their users and communities can far more effectively put them in touch with the Net and help them to use it than the IPL could ever hope to. *People can only learn where they are.*

Look and Feel: Design and Dicta

An overarching theme of the early discussion about what the IPL should and would be was to make it a "place" where people could come and find things, relax and read, congregate, and so on. The metaphor of a physical library was so strong it was often unspoken; it was taken for granted, and people would talk about the planned IPL in much the same way they would a physical library. Metaphor turned out to be one of our best friends—the more we were able to discuss things in terms of rooms and services and places found in libraries, the easier the work got and the more ideas we generated.

The importance of a sense of place in an inherently placeless environment should not be overestimated. It cuts to the heart of what a library is and what it means in a distributed world: a refuge, a stable island in a sea of chaos, an organizing force. It also conveys continuity and durability.

This metaphor formed the backdrop for conversations about what the IPL would actually look like. We had a desire (in fact, it was more like a need on our own part) for stability and place, but we also recognized that a great many people would be coming with low connectivity, using non-graphical browsers such as Lynx, or with image loading turned off for speed reasons. Therefore, we decided to go with a design that relied mainly on text. We were particularly thinking here of people (especially international users) with slow connections. It came as a pleasant surprise, then, when we received many e-mail messages from blind users praising our text-rich design. Software that vocalizes text on the screen doesn't work with images, and so our site was ideal for their use.

There were numerous impassioned discussions about design and consistency during the building period. There was strong sentiment both for consistency across the library and for separate departments, or divisions as they were called, to be able to design specifically for their users and based on their own ideas. The middle ground here was to let all groups experiment for several weeks, trying out different designs and then taking the best or combining various elements to create a single look and feel for the library. This approach worked (though not without continuing debate), and produced the first set of design dicta and a template. It's fairly simple, but therein lies its power. The point of the template and the dicta that lay behind it was to provide "wallpaper and carpeting," a basic look for all IPL pages. This freed people from thinking about design to think more about content. The page was designed to be simple—quick and easy to load and unobtrusive—yet to provide structure and information.

The logo and name of the library appear at the top of each page, so it is immediately clear that you're in the IPL, and equally clear when you've left. All pages start with a first-level heading and end with a standard footer incorporating the name of the library, the URL, an e-mail address, and the date the page was last updated. Just above that are links back up through the hierarchy of the library, sending people, level by level, up to the division home page and the library's home page (called the Main Lobby, to reinforce the building metaphor). Some pages also have a "You may also wish to see" link, suggesting related IPL sites.

All IPL pages must comply with these dicta, with a very few exceptions, such as the home page and divisional main pages (Reference, Services, Education) which can incorporate graphics. Each of these pages, though, has a text-only version in addition to the full-graphical-splendor pages. The Youth Division (and later, Exhibits) was granted a blanket exemption—they made a compelling argument that children required larger text, color, more graphics, and big buttons to click on. Their designs are based on the dicta as practical, but also reflect these needs.

The Youth and Exhibits pages also have a larger, color version of the IPL logo. That logo was also designed to be simple, easy to load, and distinctive. The small logo, which appears on the other pages, is a grayscale .GIF file of only 1K. Over time, other versions of the logo have been designed for various projects and resources. It has proved to be quite flexible; these other versions play with color but maintain the same structure and design to permit individuality within consistency.

The main lobby went through several designs. The first listed all IPL divisions and resources with lengthy descriptions. These descriptions (apparently more for our benefit than anything else)

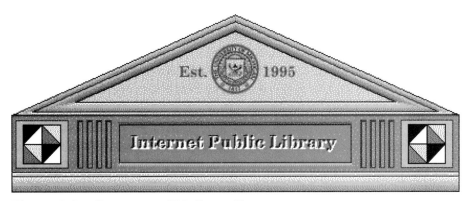

Figure 1-1.   **Prototype IPL Front Page**

vanished, but the architectural device above it remained (see Figure 1-1).

In retrospect, this was obviously intended to convey stabililty. Shortly before we opened, it was replaced by the design shown in Figure 1-2, similarly architectural but meant to resemble a plaque.

This design persisted for over two years. Many discussions arose after that time about changing it, but it didn't happen until mid-1997, when an updated home page, designed by Robert Mann and shown in Figure 1–3, was implemented.

Discussions about design, especially the front page, have often verged on the emotional. There seems to be real passion about "look and feel," which is not surprising. To the world, this is who we are, our public face, and the first impression people take away. We are confronted by a multiple challenge: we need to be interesting and inviting (which might mean changing designs and using more graphics) but we also wish to emphasize consistency (which would argue for few changes). Inertia also plays a role here, but we have opted for more superficial graphical and design changes and have worked harder on adding new resources and growing existing ones instead.

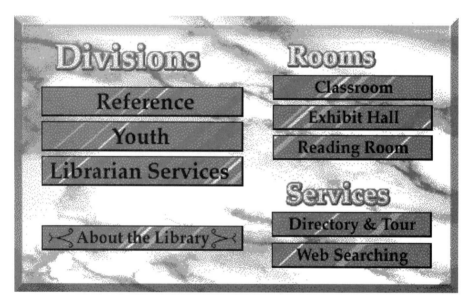

Figure 1-2.   Original IPL Front Page

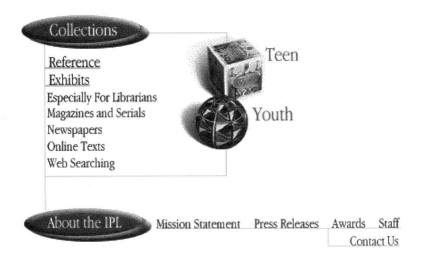

Figure 1-3.   New IPL Front Page

THE REST OF THE BOOK

I can't tell you how pleased I am to be able to share what is to come with you. In the chapters that follow, some inventive, talented people tell you much more about what they and many others have done within the IPL, and they provide some great ideas for things you can do too. David Carter's chapter on collection building and maintenance contains just the right mix of practicality and vision. Schelle Simcox tells about our efforts in building original resources, many of which she helped to foster and develop, which reflects her creativity and energy. Sara Ryan tells about our efforts and projects for young people—her passion and special gift. Nettie Lagace writes about the creation and development of the first general-purpose library reference service for a global population, a service she poured her heart and soul into and made a tremendous success. Finally, I round it out by sharing some thoughts and ideas about the economic and financial aspects of life in this new information world.

Working with each of these people has been a singular privilege for me, and you're about to see why. Enjoy.

Chapter 2

Building Online Collections

David S. Carter

As originally conceived, the IPL was not going to have any collections. In retrospect, this position is somewhat ironic, as the IPL's collections, with over 20,000 items, are one of the most visible and most frequently used components of the IPL Web site. But back in its infancy, the IPL was designed around library *services*, not "stuff." We were going to provide reference services, youth services, educational services, and services to library professionals; but we didn't need "stuff." The Internet itself would be our collection, the search engines and spiders our catalog.

It wasn't too long before we realized what a wrong notion that was. As we attempted to translate reference work to a networked environment, we realized the importance of having carefully chosen reference resources at hand when answering questions. To rely solely on Internet search engines, spiders, and sites like Yahoo in answering questions would be like going to a different room and looking through every book for an answer each time a new question was asked, instead of just grabbing the *World Almanac* (or a like source) from the nearby shelf of frequently used reference books. Worse, because the search engines and spiders were designed to deal with everything on the Internet at a fairly basic level, there was none of the organizational or evaluative added value brought to a library collection by professional librarians. It became apparent to us that a collection of Internet reference resources, selected and organized by professionals (and professionals-in-training) would be a good idea. It also made sense to us that, if we were going to go through all the trouble of putting together such a collection, we might as well share the fruits of our labor with the rest of the world by making this collection available via the IPL Web site. Thus was the IPL Ready Reference collection born.

When the IPL opened, the collections consisted of approximately 200 items in Ready Reference, all hand-coded into HTML pages, plus a handful of Shakespeare texts linked from a Shakespeare page. Today the IPL collections number over 20,000 items, covering not only reference and Shakespeare, but also associations, newspapers and serials, online texts, Native Americans, and the interests of kids and teens.

NINE STEPS TO BUILDING A COLLECTION

Since the beginning I have been involved with the construction and maintenance of all of the IPL's collections, either actively or in an advisory capacity. My experience has led me to develop a model of steps that should be taken, or at least considered, in the process of developing a collection of Internet resources. The details of these nine steps make up the majority of this chapter.

In all honesty, I have never actually followed these steps when putting together a collection! The collections I have been directly involved in creating were done before I came up with this model; what you are about to read is the result of many hard lessons learned. However, others at the IPL creating collections have been exposed to versions of this model, and have had a high degree of success in their efforts.

Step 1: Define Your Collection

Deciding what sort of Internet resources you want in your collection is the first step in building a successful collection. You could decide to try to collect everything, but that would be insane (look at Yahoo!). Instead, it is probably better to focus your collection on a project that is more manageable, both in terms of creation and maintenance.

The three factors you should consider when determining the shape of your collection are subject, scope, and audience. These factors should be informed by your situation, in terms of your library's strengths and weaknesses in its general collections, your library's mission and goals, and the knowledge and subject expertise of the persons who will be working on the project.

1. **Subject.** This is probably the most straightforward decision to be made. Often the subject for your collection will be chosen (or even dictated) by your library. For example, the staff of a natural sciences library at a university would more than likely decide to put together a collection of Internet resources relating to the natural sciences; they may even decide to break things down further, by assigning chemistry to one staff member, biology to another, and so on. Personal expertise also plays a role here; a librarian at a public library whose duties include selecting books for young adults is an obvious choice to put together a collection of Internet sites for teenagers. Personal interest is also important; your job may have nothing to do with naval matters, but if you're a person who travels around the country taking photographs of lighthouses, you're a good candidate for putting together a collection of lighthouse-related Internet sites.

2. **Scope.** You can also limit your collection by type of resource. For example, the IPL's own Associations on the Net (AON) collection covers all subjects, but only has home pages of nonprofit or not-for-profit membership-based organizations. You should also decide if your collection will only include Web resources, or if it will branch out into such things as Usenet groups and mailing lists. Another consideration is whether you'll only include freely available Net resources, or also collect those that charge a fee for use (and decide who will be responsible for that fee, the library or the patron).

3. **Audience.** There are four different audiences that you may want to aim for when building your collection: your library's

users, a subset thereof, people on the Internet who are similar to your library's users, or a general Internet audience. Your decision will not only dictate what types of and which resources you collect, but also the structure and language of your controlled vocabulary (if any) and how you present and promote your collection. It is important to note that although your library's mission may be primarily to serve your immediate users, this doesn't mean that your collection has to have exactly the same audience. The staff of the aforementioned university natural sciences library may decide that they want to put together the definitive collection of mathematics resources which includes not only sites geared toward academics and students, but also sites for kids and the general public. On the flip side, a librarian at a public library may decide that the audience for her collection will only be local small-business owners, not the entire community.

The most important thing to strive for when determining subject, scope, and audience is a balance that yields a doable and manageable collection given the staff and resources you have to work with. In all likelihood your first decisions will not be perfect, and at some point in the process you will have to return to this step and change one or more parts. The entire process is an iterative one, and you should not be afraid to revisit parts, or to make assumptions that may later need to be changed as you become more informed throughout the process.

Step 2: Determine if a Similar Collection Already Exists

If you haven't done so already, it is now time to check and see if anyone else has put together a similar collection; to scope out the "competition," or see if any even exists.

Should you find an already existing collection that closely (or even exactly) matches your plans, don't fret. You can still go ahead with your collection, perhaps changing the focus a bit. For example, if someone has already done a comprehensive mathematics collection, and done it well, you could instead decide to focus on mathematics for high school students. Or perhaps there's a collection that already does what you wanted to do, but is so lousy that you know you can do better; in which case, go right ahead.

You can also use these existing collections to help you start thinking about how to approach some of the things we'll discuss later (such as subjects, access points, features, and cataloging). See Figure 2-1 for a worksheet to guide you in evaluating existing online collections.

In any event, it may be a good idea to drop a brief e-mail note to the maintainers of similar collections, just to let them know what you'll be doing. It has been my experience that most people who maintain collections of Internet resources are pleasant, helpful folks who won't view you as competition, but rather as a colleague. And there's a good chance that they might be willing to give you some advice!

Step 3: Determine How Much Material Exists for Your Collection

At this point in the process, it is generally a good idea to do some good old fashioned Web surfing, the purpose of which is to get a feel for what kind of stuff is available for your collection. I have often referred to this activity as "gestalt info surfing," though I have no idea what that actually means. In my mind, it means starting somewhere and going with the flow, not really having any aim in mind, until you get a holistic view of the area of your collection.

When doing this "info surfing," you should keep an eye out for how the subject or topic of your collection is covered on the Internet: How does the topic break down into subtopics? Are there any "holes" in the coverage of the topic? Are any subtopics covered more or less heavily in the online environment than in the traditional print environment? Are there any identifiable Internet communities related to the topic? Are sites done largely by professionals, interested amateurs, or both? What is the intended audience of the sites, and how closely do they match the

Figure 2-1
Criteria for Evaluating an Existing Online Collection

1. What is the purpose/mission of the collection? Why does it exist?

2. What is the scope (subject and content) of the collection? Does the collection aim to be comprehensive or representative?

3. Is any value judgment (implicit or explicit) attached to items in the collection (e.g., are items rated, are only "cool" sites collected)?

4. Who provides or is responsible for the collection? Can they be contacted? How?

5. Is there an "About This Site" section? An FAQ?

6. Approximately how many items are in the collection?

7. What kinds of things are collected (e.g., Web sites, gophers, Usenet articles)?

8. What is the granularity of things collected (that is, at what level does it collect—site, page, or another level)?

9. What is included in each record?

   Examples to look for are: location, title, author, date, size, language, full text, and annotations (ask who writes them?)

10. Is there any subject access/controlled vocabulary? How are terms assigned? Is it hierarchical?

11. Can you browse the collection? How (by subject, author, title, etc.)?

   Can you search the collection?
   - Simple search (keyword/full text)?
   - Boolean? Other search structures? Proximity? Wildcards?
   - Relevance ranking? How is relevancy determined?
   - How are the results presented? Can the display be customized?
   - Is searching help available?

12. How is the collection maintained or new sites added?
   - User suggestions, robots, maintainers surfing the Web?
   - How often are updates made?

13. How is the site itself (as opposed to the collection contained therein) navigated? Are there links back to previous pages, or do you have to use your browser's Back function? Do the pages look consistent? Do you know when you have left the collection?

intended audience of your collection? And finally, how much "stuff" is out there? Also, get a feeling of where the "edges" of your collection are—that is, what sort of sites are borderline for inclusion in your collection, either due to subject or audience, and whether you'll include these borderline sites and how strict or rigid your border will be. The answers to these questions will come in handy when making decisions in later steps. Not taking the time now to get a good feel of what is out there will result in ill-informed decisions and assumptions later in the process, which means having to go back and undo work you've already done.

Once you've finished your gestalt info surfing, there's a good chance that you'll want to return to Step 1 above and reconfigure your scope, subject, and audience. Continue iterating through Steps 1, 2, and 3 until you're comfortable with the parameters of your collection and feel that there's a good likelihood of success with the technology and personnel you have available.

Step 4: Decide about Descriptive Cataloging

Now that you have a good idea of what your collection will be about and what sorts of things will go in it, it is time to figure out how you're going to keep track of all the things you select. Welcome, then, to the wonderful world of Internet cataloging.

It should be noted here that I never meant to become a cataloger. I was supposed to be a reference librarian at an academic science and engineering library; cataloging was something that just happened when the books selected were sent down to technical services in the basement and mysteriously showed up a week or two later ready to go on a shelf. But when the IPL first began to put together online collections, we quickly realized that there were no catalogers in the basement. To make matters worse, there was no Internet AACR2, no copy cataloging, no Internet name authority, nor any of the other cataloging institutions that librarians have come to rely on. In short, we were on our own.

Well, not completely on our own. After all, an Internet resource is not fundamentally different from any other chunk of intellectual work; it's just the format and instance that have changed. With this in mind, let's take a look at what sorts of things we keep track of in cataloging a book, and how those might translate over into cataloging a Web site (Figure 2-2).

Of course, the list could go on and, depending on the type of site and collection you are aiming for, could include many other types of descriptive cataloging entries (such as place of publication and frequency for an online newspaper).

Saying that a concept translates into the online world does not, however, make it identical. Let's take a look at some of these cataloging entries and the interesting wrinkles that can appear when applying them to Web sites.

Title. This is seemingly the most straightforward of all our cataloging entries; after all, nearly everything has a title, right? HTML even provides a <title> tag, which should make determining the correct title for a site even easier than in the print world. Alas, while this would be true in a perfect world, the Internet world is, as we know, far from perfect. Many Web site authors/designers don't bother to use the <title> tag, and of those who do, many use it for purposes other than the title of the site/page! Since many Internet search engines base relevancy ranking in part on words in the <title> tag, you'll find many <title> tags loaded up with laundry lists of keywords rather than actual titles of documents. Further, since the text within a <title> tag is typically displayed by browsers across the top of the browser window, many Web sites have greetings (such as "Welcome to the Coolest Salamander Site on the Internet") in the <title> tag. An additional trouble we run into with Web sites is that many of them have more than one title: you may find a site that has something perfectly sensible in the <title> tag, but there may be a different title-like string of text displayed prominently across the top of the document, a different title in the footer or an About This Site page, and yet a different title in the press release that brought the site to your attention in the

Figure 2-2.
Comparison of Descriptive Cataloging Points
for Books and Web Sites

Book	Web Site
Title	Title
Author (Statement of Responsibility)	Author/Webmaster
Publisher	Publisher? Host?
Date Published	Date Last Updated; Date Checked
# of Pages; Dimensions	Size (in Kbytes)
Call Number	URL(s)
Illustrations, Other Special Features	Inline Images, Applets, Multimedia
Table of Contents, Index	TOC, Index, Searchable
Language	Language(s)
Accession #	Record #

first place. What's a poor Internet cataloger to do? As always, my recommendation is to go with what makes the most sense. Let's stop for a moment and consider the purpose of keeping track of the title: we want it to serve as an identifier for the resource, and if possible to give some indication of the content of the resource. Because we want the title to identify the resource, we should take the title from the resource itself. No making up titles, or taking titles from press releases, or using what somebody else calls it. If you cannot find the words you want to use for the title on the resource itself, then don't use it. Typically then you'll want to take your title from the <title> tag, a prominent header tag (preferably an <h1> or <h2>tag) or from text represented in a prominent inline image header (and one would hope its <alt> tag). So what if all of these are different, or don't exist? Then we go to the second purpose of the title, to serve as some indication of the content, and choose the title that makes the most sense or is most descriptive.

In this discussion, we've been assuming that there can only

be one title. While this is often the case, in an electronic environment there's no reason why a resource cannot have more than one title, or different types of titles. All IPL collections make use of at least two titles: a Display Title and a Sort Title. The Display Title is used when presenting the resource on the Web site for the users, and can contain any sort of thing, including escape characters or diacritics, for example. The Sort Title is used for internal computational purposes: it cannot contain leading articles (the, an, a) and must begin with a capital letter, thus making sorting alphabetically so much easier; nor may it contain special characters, so numbers are often spelled out. And the Sort Title is used instead of the Display Title for determining index terms for searching. The IPL Online Texts collection makes use of two additional title types: a Series Title, so that users can easily access books or stories or articles by series (for example, Sherlock Holmes); and a nebulous Alternate Title, where I include things like title translations, common titles, uniform titles, alternate spellings, and the like.

Author/statement of responsibility. Here is another entry that, on the face of things, should be fairly straightforward. Everything has to be created by somebody, correct? But it is amazing how many Net resources you'll run across for which it is very hard to determine who the responsible party is. Some Web site authors don't identify themselves, or they identify themselves only with an e-mail address, or you may have to go digging three or four levels deep within a site to find an author's name. As with other types of resources, authors of Net resources can be individual or corporate. To make matters more confusing, often the party responsible for creating the resource has nothing to do with making the resource available online. To top things off, the line between author and publisher on the Web can often become blurred, or they may be one and the same. Take for example a typical item found in the IPL Online Texts collection: A Tale of Two Cities, originally written by Charles Dickens, prepared in electronic form and edited by Judith Boss, proofread by several persons, many of whom may be unidentified, made available as part of Project Gutenberg (which is run by Michael Hart), and finally made available over the Internet via numerous Project Gutenberg sites all over the world. As you can see, there are many potential "authors" and responsible parties for the resource. You may decide to keep track of all of them, or not. The IPL Online Texts collection keeps track of only the persons involved in the creation of the original work (such as authors, illustrators, editors, translators), in this case Charles Dickens, and the source of the electronic version, in this case Project Gutenberg.

Often a Web site will have numerous individual authors, some identifiable, some not. It is generally best in these circumstances to try to determine a corporate author and/or a Webmaster who is responsible for either the content and/or the maintenance of the Web site.

In addition to keeping track of a name for an author/responsible party, it is also helpful to try to ascertain an e-mail address for purposes of contacting someone about the site, both for the use of your patrons, and for possible assistance in collection maintenance (see Step 9 below).

Keeping track of author information for Web sites serves multiple functions: as an access point, as an identifier, as contact information, and as an aid in establishing authority for content. Keeping these functions in mind when selecting what author attributes you want to enter will help greatly.

Publisher/host. One interesting aspect of the Internet is how easy it is for anyone to publish material. These days, anyone with an America Online account can put together a Web site and make it available to everyone on the Net. So in one sense, AOL is the publisher of all of these individual home pages. But is it really the same sense of publishing that we are used to thinking about? Probably not, since AOL has no (or very little) control over the content of these sites; AOL is much more of a printer than a publisher. But then there are numerous areas of

America Online which AOL specifically and purposefully makes available, for which it is at some level responsible and thus acts much more like a traditional publisher. Ready for another headache? Available via America Online is a weekly Spider-Man "cybercomic." This cybercomic has an author, illustrator(s), and an editor—all easily identifiable persons. It is part of the Marvel Comics Online section of AOL, for which Marvel Entertainment is responsible for the content, but it is contracted for availability with AOL. In this case, AOL serves more like a retail outlet than a publisher or a printer.

When identifying a publisher for a Web site, I tend to list a publisher only if it is identifiably separate from the author, is *knowingly* responsible for making the resource available, and lends some sort of weight to the authority of the resource. These criteria are most often satisfied in two instances: resources prepared by individuals at government agencies and made available via the agency's Web site (which happens a lot with parts of NASA, for example), or resources from faculty at academic institutions. For example, for a resource about eighteenth-century Japanese music from a professor of musicology at Flugland University I would consider Flugland University to be the publisher; but for a site about Hostess baked goods by a student at the same university, Flugland would not be considered a publisher, as the powers-that-be at Flugland University are only making server space available to the student. (The powers-that-be may not necessarily know what the professor is doing either, but they are at least responsible for the professor's employment.) There are other instances where a publisher is identifiable and appropriate—for example, the IPL's Presidents of the United States resource (www.ipl.org/ref/POTUS/), where the site's creator and maintainer, Robert Summers, would be considered the author, and since it is an official part of the IPL Web site, the Internet Public Library should be considered the publisher.

We have also seen the movement of traditional publishers into the Internet. Thus articles written by reporters for the *New York Times* that appear on the *New York Times*'s Web site would probably be considered to have been published by the *New York Times*. It will be interesting to watch the development of Internet resources to see if the traditional concept of publisher becomes something akin to a reliable brand name, offering a certain amount of authority.

Dates. Traditional library cataloging is generally concerned with one date: when the resource in question was published. Sometimes there is an accession date, but that is about it. With the Internet, this concept flies right out the window. Not only are most Web sites constantly changing, but in most cases it is impossible to determine when the site first came online. For the IPL collections, we keep track of three dates: accession date, modification date (when we last modified the item record, which happens often for a variety of reasons), and the date we last checked the URL to see that it was valid. The databases are designed so that these dates are all kept track of automatically. For materials that are digitized versions of printed works, you may want to keep track of three separate dates: the date the work was originally published, the date of the edition used to make the electronic version, and the date that the electronic edition was first published.

URL. In addition to a main URL location for the resource, you may also wish to keep track of mirror sites (same content copied to other sites around the Internet), associated sites (like parent sites for subsections), or even former URLs when the resource moves.

Inlines. If a site requires and/or makes use of embedded multimedia technologies (such as QuickTime, Shockwave, Java, RealAudio), it may be helpful to let your users know before they visit, either because they may be looking for sites that use those extras, or purposefully avoiding them (I, for one, despise sites with embedded background music).

Features. Is the site searchable? browsable? Is there a site map? an index? a bibliography/"Webliography"?

Language(s). If your collection is multilingual, it's always a nice idea to let your users know if they'll be able to understand what they read when they get there.

Record #. Having a unique record number field for each item may be useful when you reach the point of making your database accessible over the Web. This may be a simple accession number, or be a bit more keyed to content.

Other things specific to your type of collection. The above points are just basic catalog items that you may want to keep track of in most situations. There are other things that may make sense depending on the type or format of things you are collecting. For example, the IPL Online Newspapers collection keeps track of place of publication (city, state, country, region) for the newspapers; the Associations on the Net collection keeps track of the geographic scope of the association (local, national, international).

Generally, I tend to err on the side of keeping track of too much information rather than not enough. It is easier to keep track of a little piece of information for each site as you go than it is to be 1,500 items into a collection, discover that you really wish you had been keeping track of it, and have to go back and look up that information again.

I realize that the above discussion, and the discussion to follow, may be driving some of the catalogers among you positively nuts. But the Internet is still a very fluid medium; thus we need to think in terms of "suggestions" rather than rules. Remember, it literally took centuries from the invention of the codex form to the development of AACR2—long enough for the form to become stable and for librarians to fight their internal wars. Add into the mix that the Internet allows for tens of millions of different publishers and styles, rather than the relative handful we've had to deal with in the physical world, and perhaps suggestions will be the best that we can ever do.

Step 5: Plan Your Subject Access

Traditional library catalogs have offered three points of access: author, title, and subject. All three were access points to the card catalog, with books shelved first according to subject (typically LC or Dewey numbers), then by author within a subject, then by title within an author, thus providing the library user with an adequate means to find a known item or browse to find an item on a particular topic.

DECIDING HOW MANY ACCESS POINTS

I'm a big fan of providing multiple access points to collections, particularly online collections. Different people have different ways of finding information, so the more access points that you offer as an option to the user, the greater the likelihood that your patrons will be able to find what they're looking for. However, over the past three years that I have been dealing with online collections, I've noticed two interesting phenomena.

First, there is the *Complexity Problem*. As more access points are added to a collection, and as these access points themselves increase in complexity, the complexity of the underlying technology (that is, database structure) becomes geometrically more complex. Most IPL collections offer two points of browsing access—by title (uncontrolled,[1] one-dimensional[2]) and by hierarchical subject (controlled, two-dimensional)—which necessitates the use of two relational databases (one for the item records, and one for the subject headings). The Native American Authors collection, to date the most complex of the IPL's collections, offers browsing access via author (controlled, one-dimensional), tribe (controlled, one-dimensional) and by work (controlled, one-dimensional), and requires four interrelated databases to manage: one for the item records, one for the tribe names, one for author information, and one for bibliographic records for the works.

Second, there is the *Access Paradox*. Simply put, the more access points you offer to the collection, and the more control, organization, and structure you give those access points, the greater the intellectual distance between the user and the sites in the collection. The simpler and fewer the choices, the quicker users can get to the information (whether it is the correct or proper information is another story). So the mere act of adding points in and of itself creates an access barrier. The delicate balancing act of providing the right level and amount of access to an online collection is one of the major feats in creating a good online collection.

Browsing via a subject hierarchy is one of the most popular modes of access to an online collection. Choosing and implementing a browsable hierarchy is one of the core challenges to the successful development of an online collection. Thus I spend the majority of the remainder of this section on that topic.

The important thing to remember is that browsing through a subject hierarchy over a Web site is an inherently different experience for the user than browsing through books arranged on a shelf according to subject. An online browser is limited to seeing only those items at a given point in the hierarchy at a given time; the user cannot simply look to the left or right, or across the aisle, and get a feeling for the gestalt of the arrangement of the items, or see similar items that may open up new avenues of exploration. It is very easy for an online browser to get lost within a hierarchy.

So by necessity browsing subject hierarchies and systems need to be less complex than their physical counterparts. Now, I am by no means an expert on the subject, but my years of practical experience have led me to develop some rules of thumb for creating online browsing hierarchies.

The 10-by-3 Rule. A browsing hierarchy is most efficient for the majority of users when it is no more than ten topics wide and three topics deep. That is, at each level of the hierarchy, the maximum number of subtopics that you want to offer to people is ten, and the furthest you want to force people to drill down in a hierarchy is three levels deep. More than ten choices, and people get confused by too many options. More than three levels deep, and people get discouraged and quit. Of course, it would be naive to think that a perfect hierarchy could be established within these constraints, and in fact there are many places within the various IPL subject hierarchies where this rule, particularly the *three deep* part, is violated. But I always feel bad when I have to violate it.

The 10-Item Rule. The most items you want to list at any place within the hierarchy is ten; more than that and the number of items to look at and choose from starts to overwhelm the user. When you get more than ten things in a spot in the hierarchy, chances are that you can form some logical groupings among the items to subdivide the categories. In a worst-case scenario, it may be necessary to revise an entire section of a subject hierarchy, especially when things do not fill in as you originally thought they would. Naturally, there is an inherent tension between the 10-Item Rule and the 10-by-3 Rule, and you'll have to use your judgment to decide which is more important in a case where they butt heads. This is probably the most violated rule at the IPL, mainly due to the fact that it is a royal pain to revise categories.

Dave's Rule of 3. Items in a collection are seldom about more than three topics. This rule came about entirely by accident. The original IPL collections allowed for only one subject heading for each item, mainly because we wanted to keep things as simple as possible. When it came time (due to a number of factors) to allow for multiple subject headings, the mechanics of database construction required me to choose a certain number of possible subject headings that could be assigned to each item; for no good reason, I chose three. As it has turned out, three was a good choice; we have found that approximately 50 percent of all items can be adequately described with one subject heading, another 30 percent with two headings, and another 15 percent with three headings. That leaves 5 percent of the items for which we would like to have a fourth heading slot available, but we just grin and suffer. I have no good evidence to support this, but I figure that an additional 4 percent of the sites could be adequately described with four headings. Why not go ahead and make a fourth slot available? Well, it would require revising both the databases and all of the scripts that process those databases for the Web interface, and quite frankly I'm not up to the task for the sake of the additional 4 percent that we would catch. Three headings work well enough for most purposes, so three it is. Now there's a whole "chicken and the egg" argument to be made here: was the choice of three subject headings fortuitous because there is something inherent in the nature of things that it works out well, or have things worked out well for three because I chose three, and would it work out just fine had four been chosen, or two or five? And is there any connection at all to the statistical fact that books in library catalogs are assigned an average of 2.5 subject headings?

Given these three rules, (the 10-by-3 Rule, the 10-Item Rule, and Dave's Rule of 3) how big a collection can be managed? Allow me to digress for a moment with a little mathematics (it's okay, I'm not only a librarian, I'm also an engineer). The 10-by-3 Rule gives us 10^3 (1,000) possible subject headings. The 10-Item Rule gives us a maximum of $1,000 \times 10 = 10,000$ slots for items. Dave's Rule of 3 tells us that there are $(1 \times 0.5) + (2 \times 0.3) + (3 \times 0.2) = 1.7$ headings per item, giving us a collection that can handle a maximum of $10,000 \div 1.7 = 5,882$ items were we to adhere strictly to the rules above. Adding another layer of depth to our hierarchy would increase the number of possible items by a factor of 10 (thus the whole geometric complexity thing).

Developing a Hierarchy

Essentially there are two approaches to choosing a subject hierarchy for your online collection: adapt an existing hierarchy or build your own. The important thing to remember when choosing or devising a subject hierarchy is that there is no such thing as a perfect subject scheme. No matter how carefully you choose your terms and construct your hierarchy, and no matter how much tinkering you do afterwards, there will always be items that don't fit well, and users who are bewildered, confused, or even genuinely upset with some of the choices you have made. So get over the idea of perfection, and instead try to develop something functional. Your subject scheme should match the needs of your users as much as possible, and should be understood by the librarians who assign the subject terms. Most of the time it does not matter which choice you make, only that you make a choice and stick to it, and try to stay as consistent as possible.

Adapting an Existing Hierarchy

At first glance, this approach is deceptively enticing; why not make use of the work that somebody else has already done? Decades of effort have gone into developing things like the Library of Congress Subject Headings (LCSH), Dewey Decimal Classification (DDC), the ERIC Thesaurus, and so on. Why should we duplicate their efforts?

Remember some of the things we talked about earlier, about the difference between browsing through an online collection and browsing through book stacks? Unfortunately, these already-developed hierarchies were not designed for online browsing. They were designed for shelving books, looking through a card catalog, using a paper-based index, or searching an online database. LCSH is fine and dandy for assigning subject terms to books, and the LC call numbers work well for shelving, but they violate the above-mentioned rules for online browsing hierarchies, making online browsing through such a system nigh impossible. Likewise, while the DDC is mostly hierarchical, and nicely follows the *10* part of the 10-by-3 rule, it complete blows apart the *3* part of the rule (Dewey numbers like 512.092073 are not uncommon). And some parts just aren't intuitive to anyone who isn't intimately familiar with it. (Quick, given the top level of Dewey—[100s]—as your starting point, where would you find calendars? Would you believe 529? It's in Horology, under Astronomy, under Natural Sciences.) You also need to take care to choose a scheme that will make sense to your users. Sure, the NASA Thesaurus is great for academia, but it is not so good for a collection of astronomy sites intended for K–12 users!

In addition, the topical coverage of human knowledge in general is quite different from the coverage on the Internet. While it is better than it was three years ago when the IPL first began, the ratio of material about Star Trek to material about Asian History is still vastly different on the Internet from the ratio in the "real" world. So a subject scheme devised for indexing journal and magazine articles may end up being filled rather lopsidedly when applied to Internet sites.

This is not to say that you shouldn't or can't adapt an existing hierarchy for your own use, just that you need to take great care, and realize that it may not be the time-saving device you think it will.

For example, the IPL has adapted an existing subject scheme, the DDC, for use in two of our collections: the Youth collection, and the Online Texts collection. In both instances, a prime motivating factor was to experiment and see how well it would work (OCLC encourages people to use Dewey for online collections for precisely this reason). For the Youth collection, using Dewey made some amount of sense, as most school and public libraries use Dewey to catalog their books, and kids might see some connection between where books are in their library and where sites are listed in the IPL: astronomy books are in the 520s at school, and astronomy sites are listed under 520 in the IPL Youth collection. For the Online Texts collection, we saw one of Dewey's most criticized weaknesses—that it focuses too much on the state of turn-of-the-century Western knowledge—as a potential strength, since a majority of the texts available on the Net are out of copyright (that is, more than 75 years old) and also tend to be from Western civilizations.

In both collections the jury is still out on the use of DDC. For the Youth collection, we limited the depth to three Dewey digits (bringing it in line with the 10-by-3 Rule) and we rewrote the subject descriptors to be a bit more kid friendly. Still, many parts are counterintuitive, especially for kids, so we have recently added a custom-made Youth subject hierarchy which exists alongside the Dewey headings. For the Online Texts collection we've put no such depth limit on the length of the numbers, which places most items many levels down the browsing hierarchy, and stretches the content out very thin (in many cases, you drill down six or so levels and only come across one lonely item). Adding a way of searching for applicable Dewey subject headings in lieu of browsing helps somewhat, but I think that we'll need to get 15,000 to 20,000 items in the collection before reaching a critical mass where we can judge the usefulness of full Dewey as a browsing hierarchy. In both collections, being able to assign more than one Dewey number to an item has caused interesting new dimensions to appear in a once-stodgy system; and getting a computer to understand DDC as a mostly hierarchical browsing structure presented a very interesting programming challenge (we had to convince the computer that 510, 501, 500.1, and 500.01, are all valid subcategories of 500, but that they are conceptually different types of subcategories).

Existing subject schemes can have uses, even if you don't adapt them whole cloth. You can adapt parts of a subject hierarchy within your custom-made hierarchy, as we have done with the DDC Table 2 (geographic regions) for the Regional and Travel section of the Serials collection, and the Our World and USA sections of the new Youth hierarchy. You can also use an existing subject scheme as inspiration in designing your own scheme. For example, the students who created our Associations on the Net collection initially looked through Gale's *Encyclopedia of Associations* to see how Gale divides associations. While the students ended up devising their own scheme, seeing how someone else had tackled the problem gave them a good place to start, and gave them ideas about what they liked and didn't like about that approach. The original IPL Ready Reference hierarchy borrowed its top level of subjects from M-Link's gopher; though the second and succeeding levels were quite different, it gave us as good a place as any to start.

Designing Your Own Subject Hierarchy

The do-it-yourself method is not going to be a walk in the park. In fact, it will probably be the most excruciating, hair-pulling, teeth-gnashing part of the whole ordeal. I wish that I could provide you with a nice step-by-step guide to creating a subject hierarchy, but despite creating or having a hand in developing the IPL's many hierarchies, I still find hierarchy development to be much more an art than a science. I can, however, supply you with a few tips and lessons learned.

First and foremost, remember your audience. Pick subject terms that will make sense to your users. If this means giving up lexicographical precision for usability, so be it. One of my all-time favorite IPL subject headings is in the Teen Division. Sara Ryan and I were trying to come up with a top-level heading for sites that were about "dating and that kind of stuff." After much teeth-gnashing, we chose "Dating & Stuff." Hey, it's not terribly precise, but it is descriptive, and our audience knows what it means!

Second, remember that scope notes can help. If there is some potential ambiguity in the controlled vocabulary term you have selected, or if there are any useful synonyms for that word, a scope note for that heading can be useful to both your users and your librarians who are assigning the subject terms.

Consider whether to adopt a strict or a loose system. This refers to how fluid your subject terms are. For example, the IPL's Ready Reference hierarchy is a strict system; after an initial period of feeling out, the hierarchy has been more or less fixed in place. Adding a new category requires a formal process and a demonstrated need, and reorganizing whole sections is a major ordeal. A cataloger who cannot find a good term to apply to an item is encouraged to pick the closest matching term. Compare this to the Online Serials hierarchy, which is loose; if I can't find a place to stick an item, I just go ahead and create a new sub-category and don't sweat the ramifications too much. Of course, the Serials collection is an inclusive rather than a selective collection, and there are no scope notes, making it both more necessary and simpler to add new categories. In contrast, the Ready Reference collection makes use of topical keywords (more about them in a bit), which mitigates somewhat the need to create new categories all the time.

When developing a hierarchical subject scheme, the path I recommend is one of familiarization, analysis, and translation. First, familiarize yourself with the subject area, and with the universe of potential items for your collection (remember what we did back in Step 3?). Then sit down and try to analyze what you have to work with—where the sites will naturally clump themselves, and how the discipline itself breaks out, either from an academic or popular perspective (or both). Finally attempt to translate what you have learned into a codified hierarchy of controlled terminology. As with most things in this chapter, this is an iterative process, so repeat as necessary.

It is probably not a good idea to devise a hierarchy by yourself, as you want to prevent your personal biases and view of the subject matter from coloring the shape of the scheme. On the other hand, you don't want to involve too many people in the process, as this can definitely be a case of too many cooks spoiling the broth. For example, five people will have five different ways of dividing up American history and they will argue about it 'til the cows come home, and yet chances are that all five methods are more or less equally valid and they just need to choose one and get on with their lives.

We have used two methods for devising subject hierarchies at the IPL, both of which have worked fairly well. For big collection projects that involve several people, we typically divide up sections (for example, Humanities, Science, Government) and give each person one or two sections. Each person develops the sections independently, then all are brought back together, comments are offered, changes are made, and eventually a system gels without too much bloodletting. Alternately, an entire first draft of a hierarchy is made by one person, it is then shown to other people for comments and suggestions, then the first person goes back to revise, shows it to people again, and continues—until the hierarchy is acceptable.

I'll say it again because it is important: There is no such thing as a perfect subject hierarchy. There just isn't. Your goal should be to devise something that is functional and that will work well for most people. You will be unhappy to some degree with your end result. Some of your patrons will complain. Some items just won't fit in your hierarchy no matter how hard you try. Tough.

Of course, nothing says that you have to use just one subject hierarchy. Hey, this is the electronic age, and we don't have to deal with putting books on shelves or filling up card catalogs. Why not allow for terms from two different subject schemes to be added to an item? You could have your own hierarchical browsing system *and* apply LCSH terms as well. In fact, this is a perfectly valid approach to take: the IPL Youth collection makes use of this approach, offering access to the collection through both a variation on the DDC and via a subject hierarchy of our own devising. Just remember the Complexity Problem and the Access Paradox, and try to keep the intellectual control of your collection manageable. More is not necessarily better.

OTHER WAYS OF DESCRIBING CONTENT

Subject hierarchies are fine and good and expedite the browsing function of a collection, but to *really* describe a resource you need to supply abstracts. In an abstract you can describe the resource in plain language, tell the user what to expect when they visit the resource, and offer tips and suggestions on how to use the resource effectively. Designing an abstract into your record structure is easy: just provide a field for an abstract in your database and you're ready to go. The actual writing of individual abstracts is the hard part. Abstract writing is an art, and a difficult art at that. Too short and an abstract is next to useless; too long and the user will never bother to read it. For IPL abstracts, we recommend that catalogers describe the resource as completely and succinctly as possible, and that they do so in a short paragraph (two or three sentences). A tall order indeed. Sometimes you'll find that a site does a good job of describing itself. Many good sites will have an About This Site section where they describe themselves. If the description is good enough, we just go ahead and copy that description into the abstract, putting it in quotes to signify that the description came from the site rather than from the IPL staff. The only real way to get good at abstract writing is to write a lot of them; while practice may not make perfect, it does make things easier.

Free-text keywords can also be useful, especially if you're using a strict subject hierarchy. Say you've got a site about black holes, but your hierarchy only gets as complex as Science—Astronomy; assigning *black holes* as a keyword can help to further differentiate the site, and additionally may be useful when the time comes later on to subdivide Astronomy. You can also use keywords to anticipate terms that your users may use to search: for a site called Canine Wonderland in a collection of sites for kids, you may want to assign keywords like *dog, doggy, puppy, pets*.

Speaking of searching, offering users the opportunity to search a collection is a good idea. Some people browse better, some search better, and some like to combine the two approaches. For IPL collections, we allow for searches to be done typically on words taken from the title, author, subject headings, keywords, and the abstract.

The problem with putting a search engine on top of your collection is your users' expectations. Because they have been conditioned by full-text Internet search engines like Alta Vista and HotBot, they will expect the search engine on your collection to behave the same way. Sure, you can try to explain that they are searching on document surrogates for the sites, not the full text of the entire contents of the site, but sadly most will not appreciate the distinction. How many times have you read articles in the popular press that try to compare Yahoo, which is a search directory, with other search engines? Invariably I want to reach into the page and give the author a good slap upside the head for trying to compare apples and oranges!

ALTERNATE WAYS OF PROVIDING ACCESS

Sometimes the nature of a collection dictates that subject is not the best way of providing access. The best IPL example is the Online Newspapers collection. Browsing access is provided by title and by place of publication, rather than a subject hierarchy, which would make very little sense for this type of collection. Instead of containing an abstract, each record contains a listing of which features/sections (such as Local News, International News, Business, Editorial, Sports, Entertainment) are available in the online edition. The trick is to think about how your users are likely to want to access your collection and go from there.

Step 6: Build Your Database (or Pot-o-Stuff)

Now that you've figured out what you want to collect and how you want to describe it, it's almost time to go out and start finding things. But first, you need to prepare a place to put things once you've found them. You also need to decide how you will go about the process of finding and adding things—especially with respect to division of labor if the collection is to be the product of more than one person. There is a degree to which these two concerns influence each other, and if push comes to shove I always recommend fitting the technology to the way you will work rather than forcing people to work around the demands of the technology.

Choosing a Database Program

In all likelihood you will want to store your item records in some sort of database. The type of database you choose should be largely influenced by the projected size of your collection.

For a collection whose size will not exceed 100 items, I recommend forgoing a database and instead putting things on one or more HTML pages. The time you spend in building and maintaining the database, plus dealing with all the database-to-Web headaches, will not justify the extra information management features that a database can supply; most people can get a grasp on managing 100 items without too much technical assistance.

If you're unfamiliar with HTML and are worried about having to deal with it, don't be. Despite all the horror stories you may have heard, HTML is nothing to be afraid of; compared to something like AACR2, HTML is a snap. I am a big fan of coding directly in HTML, but there are many programs out there that can deal with generating HTML pages from a word processor–like interface (for example, Microsoft FrontPage and Claris Home Page). And if your collection is part of a larger library-wide Web development effort, there's a good chance that you can foist off the page design aspects to whomever is in charge of that.

For a collection of between 100 and about 5,000 items, your best bet is to opt for a commercial personal database product (such as Microsoft Access or FileMaker Pro), which provides a good deal of database power while still being user-friendly enough not to keep you up nights. These programs can also be used effectively for managing collections of over 5,000 items, but you'll start to run into some performance issues as the number of items gets too big. At some point you may want to consider converting to one of those big, nasty, full-featured, mega-database programs (Oracle or its ilk). Of course, these programs tend to be rather expensive and complicated as hell, but if you have the technical expertise and the need for speed, you may want to consider one if your collection gets too large and unwieldy.

SELECTING A DATABASE PROGRAM: AN IPL EXAMPLE

At the IPL we use various FileMaker Pro (FMP) databases to manage our collections; each collection has its own database (or collection of databases) which is individually managed. Using FileMaker Pro has had its good and bad points, with the good outweighing the bad, perhaps because it fits the convoluted work structure of the IPL fairly well. At this point it might be illustrative to look at some of the reasons why the IPL uses FileMaker Pro, not as an advertisement for Claris, but rather as an example of the sorts of things to look for in a database.

1. Of course, there is the issue of cost. Normally, a single-user license for FMP costs about $300 (a single-user educational license runs about $100), which is quite reasonable for this sort of database. However, as the University of Michigan (U of M) School of Information (SI, where the IPL is housed) already had a site license for FMP, the additional cost for the IPL to make use of it was zero. For a cash-strapped organization like the IPL, the availability of a good-quality database product for no extra money is an important factor!

2. FMP is a cross-platform, Macintosh native program. The U of M campus is Mac-centric; most of the student computer labs are stocked with Macintosh computers, including the main SI student lab, and all but one of the computers in the IPL staff offices are Macs. Thus, choosing a database program that is made for the Macintosh was an important consideration. In addition, Claris makes a version of FMP for Windows which has nearly all the functionality of the Mac version and can share the same database files, thus also making it possible for those involved with the IPL who use Windows machines to access the databases.

3. FMP can be networked and multiuser. FMP databases can be shared over a variety of different networks, including AppleTalk and TCP/IP networks, and setting up a database to

be shared is as simple as selecting an option from a pull-down menu. Since we have numerous students and staff who may want to use an IPL database at any time from anywhere on campus, this feature is vital. The latest version of FMP (version 4) includes direct Web publishing abilities which allow anyone with access to a Web browser to perform browsing, searching, and data entering functions over the Internet from anywhere in the world.

4. I was already familiar with FMP prior to our deciding to use it for the IPL, which meant that there wouldn't be a big learning curve for me to get up to speed on using it. As most of the collection management duties would be falling on my shoulders, my familiarity with the program was a definite plus.

5. FMP is a fairly easy program to use. If you can point and click with a mouse and type on a keyboard, you can navigate and enter data into an already existing FMP database with little difficulty. Creating new and modifying existing databases is a bit trickier, but it is still fairly straightforward and it follows standard Macintosh interface guidelines.

6. FMP has some very nice functions, including scripting, drag-and-drop editing, spell checking, automatic data entry, easy importing and exporting of data, and quasi-relational database structures.

For the size and type of collections that the IPL has, and for our style of work, FMP fits our needs quite nicely. However, this is not to say that there aren't some drawbacks to using FMP.

FMP's scripting language and environment is really screwy. I get the feeling that the FMP programmers were designing a scripting language that could be used by people without programming experience, but for those of us who are used to programming or are experienced with database design, the scripting is bizarre.

There are numerous options for directly integrating FMP databases with a Macintosh Web server. However, the IPL uses Apache Web servers on UNIX machines, for which no direct integration with FMP is available. This means that in order to make the content of our collections available, we have to go through a number of convoluted, homegrown steps (this problem is discussed further in Step 8 below). This is not an ideal situation, but the lack of a good, cheap, easy-to-use, UNIX-based database, or of the possibility to use a Mac Web server effectively, makes a situation like this unavoidable for us.

Step 7: Select Items for Your Core Collection

WHERE TO FIND THINGS AND WHAT TO LOOK FOR

Now it's finally time to start putting things into your database. There's a good possibility that you already have a kernel of a collection, perhaps a basic HTML page from your library's Web site with a few applicable links, or a bunch of bookmarks that you've been collecting. You've also undoubtedly stumbled across several good things while you were working through the earlier steps in this process. Fairly obviously you should begin with these items, then work on finding more things.

When tackling the process of finding items for your initial population, it is a good idea to have some sort of plan. Begin by assuming that your collection will not be perfect, and your collection will never be complete. What you want to aim for is an opening collection that both is useful and shows the potential for your collection in the future. For people who are working on building new IPL collections, I tell them to aim for an initial set of 100 to 200 items before opening.

Good places to begin looking for items for your collection are the other collections that you may have identified in Step 2. This is a process that I like to call collection mining. If these collections are any good, you can add them as a whole to your own collection, and then go back at some later point to identify the things that would be useful to add individually to your collection. If the other collections really stink (for example, lack of or bad organization, no abstracts, lack of maintenance), but they still have pointers to some good resources, go ahead and use these collections to identify the good sites.

For your next step, it's time to plunder your good friend Yahoo. Find the categories of Yahoo that relate to your collection. Most Yahoo categories have a subsection called Indexes, where you will find non-Yahoo indexes to Web sites for that category; mine and plunder these as you did the collections you found earlier. Now look at the individual Web sites that Yahoo has listed; with a little experience you'll be able to look at the brief Yahoo description and decide if it's worth your time to click on it and check it out.

An important thing to keep in mind when using Yahoo is their criteria for inclusion: if, in the mind of the Yahoo site "reviewer" (I use the term very loosely) the Web site is likely to be of interest to *more than one person*, it gets in. A looser collection development policy there has never been! It is also important to note that most of the descriptions you read in Yahoo are written by the person who submitted the site, which in most cases is someone involved in creating the site. Caveat surfor.

Depending on your collection, it may also be worth your time to go to your favorite Internet search engine (Alta Vista, HotBot, or Northern Lights, for example) and try a series of carefully chosen searches. For example, when building the initial collection for the IPL's Associations on the Net collection, the students involved went to Alta Vista and used Boolean phrases like *physics and (association or society or institute)* to uncover the home pages of applicable associations.

As part of your initial plan of attack, you will want to aim for some amount of "representational comprehensiveness," or, in other words, a little bit of everything for every part of your collection, rather than focusing heavily on one area and letting the others languish. If you have developed or are using a hierarchical subject scheme, a good way to accomplish this is to try to get a certain number of sites for each individual level of your hierarchy; three to five items is generally a good number, depending on the complexity and breadth of your scheme.

One important thing to realize is that no matter how well you have designed your subject scheme (or other access points) *it will break down* as you find things you want to put in it. And it will happen sooner rather than later. I can almost guarantee that, at some point within the first 20 items you try to add, at least one will not fit into your carefully designed hierarchy. And more will pop up as you continue. There are two ways of dealing with this: force the item into some place where it doesn't really fit, or redesign a section of your hierarchy. Both are valid ways to go, but if you find yourself forcing more than a handful of things, that's probably a good indication that you need to rethink your subjects. Don't be afraid to revisit Step 5 at some point during your process of "populating" your collection.

EVALUATION

The question that I am most often asked is, "How do I evaluate online resources?" I must admit that this question has always puzzled me, because when it comes right down to it, you *already know* how to evaluate online resources. The same basic criteria that librarians have always used to evaluate information resources are applicable to online resources as well.

These criteria fall into three categories: content, access, and user appropriateness. Content, of course, is the most nebulous of the three, covering such areas as authority, scope and depth of coverage, accuracy, currency, and bias. Access covers such areas as the container (book, sound recording, and so on), organization, physical aesthetics, and cost. User appropriateness covers such areas as reading level, tone (for example, scholarly versus popular), and user interest. Many librarians have written at length about these topics, so I won't rehash them here. Instead, I'll spend the rest of this section discussing the additional wrinkles that evaluating online resources adds to the mix.

People get tripped up in the evaluation of online resources because, given the nature of the medium, it is often much harder to determine such things as authority for a Web site than it is for a book. A librarian now has to think much harder about the authority of a resource, and possibly decide whether authority even matters. And sometimes you just have to make assumptions.

Often you can gather clues based on the profession of the person or persons who have written the information or who are making it available. A physics resource, written by a professor of physics at a major research university and made available from his or her academic department's Web server, is probably more authoritative than a resource written by a nameless AOL user.

I think that one movement we will see on the Net in the next few years is the evolution of traditional publishers into something akin to name-brand Web publishing. While this is not publishing in the traditional sense, publishers will still take on the functions of commissioning and editing resources and making them available on the Web. Let's face it, people are much more likely to trust something with the name "Britannica" or "New York Times" on it than they are the same information coming from a site maintained by Jane Q. Public. We will also begin to see new publisher-like entities gain a reputation solely on the Net.

As an example, when I add a text from Project Gutenberg (PG) into the IPL's Online Texts collection, I assume that the text I'm adding is a complete version, without any deliberate or accidental errors or omissions. I can assume this, because I know something about the process that texts go through to be accepted into PG (which includes copyediting, proofreading, and revision), and because PG has gained a reputation over the years for providing texts at a certain level of quality.

Another aspect of evaluating Web sites which presents different issues is that of navigation: sidebars, frames, search features, site maps, and so on. Let's face it, there is a *lot* of bad site design on the Web, most of which is caused by two factions: 1) people with no clue about information design who try to do things that "look cool," and 2) people with a background in traditional graphic design who try to do things the same way in the online environment. This is still a new information environment, and people are experimenting all the time with new ways to present information. But basically you should always be able to tell where you are in a site, how to get back from whence you came, where you are likely to want to go to find something in a site, and when you are leaving a site. Since different people think about and access information differently, multiple access points are always a plus. Whenever I'm evaluating a site, I try a simple test: I think of a piece of information that I'm likely to find at that site, and then I try to find it. (A negative answer in this instance can be as useful as a positive one; if I can quickly determine that the information I'm after is not on the site, that's just as good an indicator of good site design as actually finding the information quickly.) If you, as an information professional, have a hard time figuring out a site, what chance will your users have?

Concurrent to site design is a site's aesthetic qualities. As in the traditional world, a "less is more" approach generally holds up pretty well. Simplicity and functionality often go hand-in-hand. Does the site you're evaluating really need five animated GIFs of cartoon frogs hopping around? Or annoying background music that you cannot turn off? Or frames up the wazoo? Or a 215K background image? Or navy blue text on a shocking pink background? Also keep in mind that every image, every Shockwave plug-in, every Java applet, is an access barrier for your users, most of whom are accessing the Internet via a 28.8 bps modem.

One true test of a site's worthiness is whether it can be successfully navigated and used with image loading turned off in your browser. You'd be amazed at how many sites become absolutely incomprehensible without their images, and how many Web designers don't include basic things like <alt> tags for images and text equivalents of image maps.

It is always useful to recall Sturgeon's Law: 90 percent of everything is crap.[3] On the Web, because of the lack of editorial vestment, it is probably closer to 99 percent. (Luckily, there's so much stuff, that the remaining 1 percent provides a lot of useful content.)

Of course, the ultimate question when evaluating a Web site for inclusion in your collection should be, "Does it meet the criteria of the collection policy?" In some situations, especially for a collection that seeks to be comprehensive, this is a no-brainer. For example, take the case of the IPL's Online Newspapers collection. The collection policy states:

> The IPL Online Newspapers collection lists online versions of print-based newspapers. In addition to traditional local and national newspapers, it also lists official and student-run newspapers from colleges, universities, and primary and secondary schools. To be considered for inclusion, the online version of the newspaper must include some significant amount of articles and other information that is free to the general public.

So if it looks like and quacks like an online newspaper, it goes in.

On the other hand, the IPL Teen Division's policy calls for much greater scrutiny on behalf of the person collecting sites:

> The collection of the Teen Division of the Internet Public Library is developed for teenagers ages 13–19 and their parents, teachers, and anyone else interested in information directed to and about teenagers and young adults. Material used and sites recommended are chosen based on their appropriateness for the subject matter and should be written and maintained by an authoritative source. The information should be current, accurate, and presented in an objective and well-organized manner. While the resources may not necessarily be aimed specifically at teens, their contents should be of interest and useful to these age groups.

The Teen Division policy is discussed further in Chapter 4.

For collection development that requires an evaluative component, ask yourself, "Will it be worth the time for users of this collection to take a look at this resource?" Because when it comes right down to it, we must take a "Siskel and Ebert" approach to our collections: thumbs up or thumbs down. It either goes in or it doesn't.[4] Sure, we can use abstracts, ratings, or other methods of indicating degrees of worthiness, but as librarians, our inclusion of any type of resource in our collections indicates some level of worthiness for that resource.

Step 8: Make the Database Available to the Public

It's great to have your collection sitting in a well-designed database, but it does your patrons no good if they can't get at it. While there are many methods for making a database of Web resources available to the public (such as including the items as MARC records in an online catalog), we'll be considering for methods for using the most popular delivery system: making the database available over the World Wide Web.

METHOD 1: DIRECT ACCESS TO THE DATABASE

If direct access is available as an option, this should be the first method you consider. Allowing the users direct access to the database via a Web-based interface has many advantages, chief among them being simplicity. There are third-party database-to-Web solutions available for most commercial databases (such as Tango for FileMaker Pro and Mac Web servers), and many databases now have their own built-in Web interfaces (such as the new FileMaker Pro 4.0). While these solutions may require a little HTML wizardry to go beyond a basic "blah" interface, usually very little or no programming knowledge is required.

Problems in using this approach are twofold: (1) If your database and Web server reside on two different platforms (as is the case with the IPL), it is highly unlikely that you'll be able to find a direct access solution. (2) If you're using a personal-level database product (for example, FMP or Microsoft Access), a large and frequent amount of use by Web patrons will quickly overload and bring your system to its knees. Both of these reasons have prevented the IPL from using a direct-to-Web approach for handling our collections.

METHOD 2: GENERATE AND OUTPUT HTML CODE FROM THE DATABASE

This method is well suited for collection sizes in the 100 to 300 items range, and it is being used rather successfully in the IPL's Especially for Librarians collection and our database of IPL press clippings. In the FMP database for the collection, each record uses a calculated field that generates the HTML code desired for the item record that appears on the Web site. We use the database's search-and-sort capabilities to get the records we want in the order we want them, and then just export the field with the HTML code. The use of the database's scripting capabilities automates this process. The file or files containing the HTML records are then moved to the correct place on the Web server, and the server's file-include capabilities are used to insert the files containing the records into a standard HTML page (which includes such things as the header, the footer, and any other explanatory copy and navigational bits) on-the-fly whenever the page is requested from the server. Again, this method requires no programming expertise, only a working knowledge of HTML and a Web server capable of handling server-side file-include commands (as most are).

While this solution works fine for a smallish collection with one-dimensional access (for example, a simple, non-hierarchical subject list), it rapidly becomes a conceptual nightmare and logistical monstrosity with a more complex collection. It is still possible, but having your database churn out literally thousands of individual snippets of HTML code is not terribly efficient.

METHOD 3A: CGI PROCESSING OF TAB-DELIMITED DATABASE OUTPUT

This is the method used most often in the IPL collections (for example, Associations on the Net, Serials, Newspapers, Youth, Teen, Native Authors). Fairly straightforward database scripting is used to export the desired fields from the records into a tab-delimited output file, with each line of the file containing one record, the fields separated by a tab character. Then a series of Perl scripts are used to do some preprocessing of the data (for example, creating some index files), and then CGI scripts (again written in Perl) are used to generate HTML pages on-the-fly as users browse and/or search the collection. While a lot of work must be done up front to get this kind of solution up and running (a process which become geometrically more complex as multiple access points are added to a collection), once it is in place the scripts can be wrapped up into a single shell script and you have an easy-to-maintain, one-step way to update your collection. It also offers easy flexibility in the presentation of your collection, as all that is required to update the look of your collection is to modify the code in a single Perl script. While any scripting or programming language can be used for a CGI solution, Perl is recommended because of its flexibility, its excellent handling of text strings, its ubiquitousness on the Net (that is, it is very easy to get help and find examples), and its cost (it's free!).

The chief drawback to this approach is that it requires programming skill. While one does not need to be a master programmer to write Perl scripts, it does require a nontrivial amount of effort to learn and practice to implement it efficiently. Also, this type of solution does not scale particularly well. As the size of your collection increases, so too does the time required for the CGI script to process your collection and deliver the desired output to the users; the time isn't too bad for the largest of the IPL collections that use this approach (around 2,000 items), but the delay would probably become noticeably annoying as the collection size approached 7,000 to 10,000 items. Additionally, each access of the CGI script requires a separate process to be started and executed by the Web server, so if a collection is too popular, the high level of usage can cause the entire server to drag and even hang. It was this last drawback in relation to the IPL's Ready Reference collection which required us to develop the next method.

METHOD 3B: SCRIPT GENERATION OF STATIC HTML PAGES FROM TAB-DELIMITED DATABASE OUTPUT

The most popular section of the IPL has been, and will undoubtedly continue to be, the Ready Reference collection. This popularity became a technical problem when we migrated that collection from static Web pages to an on-the-fly CGI approach, as the high usage rate of the collection caused the constant access of the CGI scripts to completely bog down the server. While the optimal solution would have been to buy more and faster Web servers, a lack of funds for making that solution a reality necessitated a different approach. A modified version of the CGI browsing script for the Ready Reference collection is now used to create a series of static HTML pages, one for each subject heading (there are 350 or so) and one for each letter of the alphabet. So, while CGI processing creates a virtual 'page' of HTML on-the-fly when a user requests it, with static generation, the HTML pages are created once by the script beforehand and then served up to the user. This approach is superior over Method 2 in that creating the pages whole-cloth out of Perl scripts offers much more flexibility than generating HTML code within the database.

METHOD 4: SEND DATABASE RECORDS TO A MORE ROBUST SEARCH-AND-RETRIEVAL SYSTEM

This convoluted method is used for the largest IPL collection, our Online Texts. In conjunction with the Humanities Text Initiative (HTI) at the University of Michigan, we've developed a system whereby the records in our FMP database are converted into an SGML file (using a special DTD [Digital Type Definition] jointly developed) and imported into the OpenText SGML server run by HTI. A set of CGI scripts (developed by HTI librarian and IPL alumnus Nigel Kerr) create the interface between the Web server and the HTI server. The advantage over Method 3 is that OpenText is a heck of a lot more robust than any of the simple Perl scripts that I wrote myself, and it can handle large collections as easily as smaller ones (in the two years that this system has been in use, the Online Texts collection has more than tripled to over 8,000 items and shows no sign of slowing down). This method is advantageous over storing everything in OpenText directly in that the user interface to FMP is far more intuitive and easier to use than OpenText's own interface. The chief drawbacks are twofold: access to a high-end search-and-retrieval system such as OpenText does not come cheap, and you need someone around who is proficient in both the operation of that system and in programming to make it work. Without the good graces of the fine folks at HTI, this solution would not be possible for the IPL.

There are undoubtedly other methods for database-to-Web delivery of collections, but those discussed above are the ones we have used (or explored) at the IPL. You are limited only by your imagination, skills, and pocketbook; but with enough skill and imagination, you should be able to develop a workable solution for delivering your collections, whatever the constraints on your pocketbook.

Step 9: Plan for Ongoing Collection Development
Now that your collection of Internet resources is up and running (and you are receiving numerous and well-deserved accolades from the public and your fellow librarians) you can rest, but not for too long! Just as for all traditional library collections, collection maintenance is an important part of keeping an Internet collection useful and relevant. In fact, because of the rapidly changing nature of the Internet, maintenance activities are probably more important for Internet collections. Imagine if one day you went looking in your library's reference collection, and overnight someone had rewritten large portions of a popular reference book; or three chapters had been removed and two appendixes had been added; or you opened the cover and found nothing but blank pages; or suddenly, partway through a book you read all the way through yesterday, you are now asked to fork over $14.95 to continue reading! Barring the case of books

being stolen, lost, or deliberately defaced, once a library buys a book it stays pretty much the same. But the same variability and instant publishing that can make Internet resources attractive in many ways can also lead to many headaches for collection maintenance. Essentially there are two parts of Internet collection maintenance: dealing with currently existing items and finding new items.

CHECKING LINKS

Link checking is the Internet equivalent of library shelf reading; it's an icky, boring job, but needs to be done periodically to ensure the integrity of your collection.

The second question I am most frequently asked is "What about automatic link-checking programs? Do any of them work?" I've looked at many of these programs over the past couple of years and all the ones I've examined basically stink. The reason for this is fundamental: programs are stupid and can only do what they're told; people are smart and can infer, make judgments, and improvise. A link-checking program can only report whether it connected successfully, and usually can tell you if it received an error message (such as 404 (DNS problem) or 403 (Site Forbidden). The programs cannot tell you *why* they were unable to connect. (Even worse, they may be able to connect, but the content at the URL may have completely changed.) Link-checking programs usually check each link only once, but most bad URLs need to be checked again (often several hours later) before a determination of a problem can be made. Also, all the link-checking programs that I'm aware of are designed to check only URLs that are hard-coded into permanent HTML pages; so if your collection is stored in a database and accessed via CGI scripts, forget it! Both Michael McClennen (our IPL system-administrator) and I have, at various times, entertained the notion of writing a useful, smart URL-checking program. Maybe we will someday, or perhaps somebody else out there will catch a clue and write something genuinely helpful. But don't hold your breath.

So how should you check for bad links? Your best weapon in the war against dead links is your users, many of whom will let you know when they cannot connect to something in your collection. You should also institute a program for comprehensive link checking that you carry out every few months (and if you happen to have a class full of library students at your disposal, so much the better!).

REVISING CURRENT ITEMS

This link checking is crucial, because once a resource has been added to your collection, chances are that at some point it will need "weeding" or revising.

The list of possible reasons is as long as a winter day in Antarctica, but they usually fall into several major areas.

Site Has Moved, with a Notice

Valid URLs change for Internet resources all the time. Polite Webmasters and resource maintainers leave a message at the old address stating the new address, and some even automatically redirect you to the new location. Sites change locations for any number of reasons, including site reorganization, a change of Internet Service Providers (ISPs), and the site getting its own domain name. (This last reason is one of the most prevalent recently, as having your own domain name now seems to be the newest Internet status symbol. (Frequently you'll find, for example, that a site at www.genericISP.com/fire-breathing-duck/ has moved to www.fire-breathing-duck.com/. Once everybody gets their own domain name, I imagine that this sort of location changing will taper off.) Dealing with moved sites is relatively straightforward, as you just have to go into the item's record and replace the old URL with the new URL. I also recommend keeping track in the database of what the old URL was; if you are also keeping access statistics for your collection, you may at some point need to know what the old location was.

Link Is Dead.

Dead links are the bane of all Internet collection maintainers. An informal survey that appeared in the July 22, 1996 issue of *WebWeek* found that somewhere between 5 and 10 percent of all external links on Web sites go bad each month; imagine the clamor if 5 to 10 percent of the books in your print collection went missing each month! Links can go dead for a number of reasons:

Site gone. Internet resources have a relatively high mortality rate, and unfortunately it seems that the good sites are often the ones to go. Sites die for many reasons, but it usually boils down to lack of money, time, or inspiration on behalf of the resource provider. Unfortunately there's not much you can do in this case, other than to delete the item from your collection, shed a small tear, and look to see if you can find anything similar with which to replace it.

Site moved, with no notice. This is one of the more insidious reasons for dead links, because it looks and acts like any of the other reasons. While simple non-consideration for users is the most common reason for this, there are other less sinister reasons as well. Common explanations are that the resource changed ISPs and the former ISP has not left up a notice for an old account, or that the university students who once housed the resource on the school's Web servers have graduated and it has moved to an ISP.

Since a site that has moved with no notice appears like any other dead link, I have developed a simple process for trying to determine if a dead link is the result of a site moving:

1. If the site is for an organization or a company with a short name, I try to guess the new location. This isn't as hard as it sounds; for example, if the link for the American Society of Fire-Breathing Ducks used to be at www.genericISP. com/asfbd/ you might try www.asfbd.org/ or www.asfbd.net/.

A company called GlobeTech, once at www.genericISP. com/globetech/ has more than likely moved to www.globe tech.com/.

2. Do a search for the resource title in Yahoo (www.yahoo. com/). This is where taking the resource title directly from the resource itself comes in handy. Put the title in quotes in the search field (so that it is searched as a single string) and see what comes up. Often you'll find the same bad URL that you have in your own collection, but frequently you'll find that the listing in Yahoo has been updated. If that doesn't work, I scroll down to the bottom of the Yahoo search results page and clink on the link to HotBot (www.hotbot.com/) which causes the same search to be executed in HotBot's Web page index; I choose HotBot because, of all the current comprehensive Web search engines, it reindexes the most often.

3. If neither of the above steps works, and if I have an e-mail address for the Webmaster or contact person for the missing site, I write off a brief, polite e-mail message inquiring what has happened. Usually this results in an undeliverable (bounced-back) message, or a reply confirming that the site is indeed gone for good. Still, it's nice to have confirmation from the source, and sometimes the person is able to tell me that the site has indeed moved, or can recommend a replacement site.

If the above process fails to turn up a new location for the site, I usually assume that it is gone for good and delete it from the collection.

Site forbidden. The 403 Site Forbidden server message is a cause of confusion to many, but it is usually the result of one of two things: a problem with directory permissions on the site's host machine (this happened to the IPL on more than one occasion in our early days), or a site that was once free to be accessed by the entire world is now restricted to users of certain machines or in certain domains. The first explanation is usually a temporary problem, the second is more than likely permanent. A quick e-mail to the site maintainer can usually clear up a temporary permission problem, but if the problem persists for several days, assume that restrictions apply and delete the site from your collection.

Temporary Technical Problems

Sometimes you cannot connect to a site because of technical problems that are out of your control, but which will clear up on their own. These include:

Server down or busy. Web servers are on the whole rather fragile things and have been known to crash temporarily, or to freeze up due to heavy traffic (which also has been known to happen to the IPL). These problems are usually fixed within a few hours.

Net congestion. That the Net gets bogged down in traffic in the middle of the day isn't news to anyone. Sometimes Net traffic is so heavy that you cannot connect to a site before your Web browser times out; most often this happens when the 9-to-5 business hours of the East and West coasts of the United States overlap. During daytime hours in North America, the United States and Canada are practically inaccessible to the rest of the world because traffic is so heavy (this is the main reason why the IPL maintains a European mirror site in Sweden). If you cannot connect to a Web site, try again—in the morning (for the East coast) or the late afternoon/early evening (for the West coast)—when traffic isn't as heavy.

Domain name server (DNS) problem. The Internet's DNS system is one of the core technologies that keeps the Net running smoothly; it's what resolves (converts) an address such as www.ipl.org to the proper IP address (141.211.203.56) so that your computer can find the site it is looking for. Temporary problems with DNS servers—either on your end, at the site's end, or somewhere in between—can result in your Web browser telling you that it cannot find the site. Ninety-five times out of 100, a DNS error for a previously fine URL is the result of a temporary difficulty. Whenever I encounter a likely DNS problem, I immediately try again to connect to the site, and if that doesn't work I try again in a few hours or the next day. Such problems usually iron themselves out.

External router problem. If you find that you cannot connect to anything in your collection, or to a significant portion, chances are that there's a problem with the router that connects your local network to the rest of the Internet. It's usually a good idea to notify your technical support staff to make sure that they know of the problem. It may also be that the site you're looking for is having a router problem, and hopefully their technical support staff will fix the problem in a few hours.

The moral of the story on temporary problems is this: Never jump to conclusions. Never assume, just because you cannot currently connect to a site, that the site is gone for good. Wait a day or two and try again before taking harsh measures.

Content Changed

In truth, for most of the items in online collections, we do hope that the content changes regularly; one of the benefits of using Internet resources is their capability to be updated constantly and to offer current information. However, sometimes sites change so much that action must be taken. Most often this occurs when a resource adds new features and the abstract should be rewritten. Sometimes a site expands in scope, in which case you may need to add to or change its subject headings. A once free site may now require a membership fee for access. In an extreme case, a site could completely change; most often this occurs when a resource moves from an ISP to elsewhere, and the old URL is now directed to the ISP's home page.

Site No Longer Relevant

It could be that nothing about the site has fundamentally changed, but the nature of your collection has, and the site no longer fits. Perhaps you started out with a collection about chemistry in general, but it has evolved into a collection of sites geared toward undergraduate college students, in which case you might want to get rid of that Chemistry Fun for Kids site.

Another possibility is that you've found a site that is not only similar to, but demonstrably better than a site already in your collection. Perhaps you added a resource that was a simple listing of home pages for churches in the United States because that was the best available at the time, but now there's a new site that is searchable, covers the whole world, covers non-Christian places of worship, and contains more information than just church name and URL. It is probably time to remove the old site from your collection in favor of the newer site; there is no reason to lead people to a resource that's inferior to a similar site in your collection.

FINDING NEW STUFF

Another question I am often asked is "How do I find new stuff for my collection?" Unlike the traditional world, where we're all comfy with our approval plans, publishers' catalogs, and the like, the Internet is too new to libraries for us to have any organized way for new resources to come to our attention. Over the last few years that I've been doing online collection development and maintenance, I've used a variety of methods for finding out about new resources that I may wish to add to the IPL collections.

Patron suggestions. Just as they can help with identifying bad links, patrons can also recommend potential resources that you may not know about. Granted, you will get a lot of *poor* suggestions from users, but for every unworthy suggestion ("Here's the URL for my photographs of Fire-Breathing Ducks!") or wish list ("You should put books by Stephen King in your Web site;

he's a very popular author and lots of people like me would like to read his books on the Internet.") you'll get a suggestion with a valid URL that will be worth at least a look.

Random surfing. Sometimes it's good just to start someplace on the Net and follow links until you find something interesting and/or useful. While this may not seem like the best way to spend your time, it usually results in finding at least one or two good things that you would not have discovered otherwise, and is worth doing for an hour or so once a month.

Fallout from other library activities. In the process of doing other parts of your job, such as answering reference questions, you're likely to come across a Web site that would make a good addition to your collection. By all means, add it. You've already gone to the trouble of identifying and evaluating the site, so why not go the extra step and add it to your database?

Print sources. The arrival of the Internet into popular consciousness has resulted in a gush of books and magazines that review Web sites. As with everything else, Sturgeon's Law (90 percent of everything is crap) applies here, but there are a couple of sources worth mentioning. My current favorites for finding new sites with reviews are *Yahoo! Internet Life* and *WebGuide Magazine*. The trouble with all of these publications is that they're written for the general public, not for librarians, so the evaluation criteria tends to be a vague notion of "coolness" and style, rather than things we librarians look for, such as usefulness, reliability, and authority. Web site reviews are also starting to appear in sources that are not dedicated to the Internet, such as newspapers and subject-specific magazines. For example, *Popular Science* now has a short column with listings for science-related Web sites.

Web sites. My absolute favorite resource for finding new sites is the Internet Scout Report, a weekly publication from the fine folks (many of whom are librarians) at the Internet Scout Project at the University of Wisconsin. To subscribe see www.scout.cs. wisc.edu/scout/report/subscribe.html. A few other Web sites also rate/evaluate other sites, but most of them have the same problem as the aforementioned print publications, with the additional wrinkle that many of them try to get the sites they review to put an award logo and link back to their site (to increase traffic and therefore advertising revenue); thus the motive and quality of their review is potentially suspect.

Another favorite resource is the What's New section of Yahoo (www.yahoo.com/new/), which contains a daily listing of every new site added to Yahoo's hierarchy. This is the closest thing to a current awareness service for Web sites, and I recommend staking out the part of the Yahoo hierarchy that is applicable to your collection and at least glancing at it every day to see what's new.

Usenet groups/mailing lists. Librarians have long known the potential of e-mail lists and Usenet groups for professional communication, and it should be no surprise that other professions have them as well. Newsgroups and listservs dedicated to specific topics are excellent sources for learning of Internet resources that practitioners are using and recommending to one another. If you're putting together a collection of physics sites, it is time to start reading those sci.physics.* Usenet groups. In addition, a few groups are solely dedicated to the announcement of new Net resources, namely comp.infosystems.www.announce and comp.internet.net-happenings. These groups can get overwhelming rather quickly, so unless you have a lot of time on your hands you may wish to apply a few judiciously chosen searches in DejaNews (www.dejanews.com/) to parse through the message contents for useful stuff.

One thing you'll probably notice is that your regular collection development activities will not result in an even distribution of new sites over the breadth of your collection. It is probably a good idea to sit down every six months or so, find the areas of your collection that are starting to look skimpy compared to others, and make a concerted attempt to find some new sites to add. (This is also a good opportunity to do other collection maintenance as well, such as checking links!)

INTERACTING WITH USERS

For the most part, your interaction with your collection's users, usually via e-mail or a feedback form, will be generally positive, or at least helpful. Users can be an essential part of identifying new resources or problems with existing resources in your collection. And there's nothing better than receiving a message from a user telling you what a wonderful job you are doing. However, a couple of types of user interaction may grate on you, so following are some brief words about them:

Border confusion. Some Internet denizens have a hard time telling where one site ends and another begins. At least once a week we get a message from someone telling us that they're having problems using something that we point to, or that there's a small factual error or typo in a site listed within one of our collections. There are two ways to deal with this: (1) send a note back to the user explaining that the site is separate from your collection and that you have no control over its contents, and suggest that they contact the Webmaster of that site; or (2) forward the message to the site's Webmaster/maintainer. IPL uses both ways, depending on the situation.

Challenges. As with all library collections, collections of online resources will eventually be challenged regarding a resource's suitability for inclusion. As with traditional challenges, your best weapons are a clear collection policy and formal challenge process; you may decide to amend/modify your library's existing policies, or draft new ones for your online collection.

One unique wrinkle to challenges in online collections is the "You link to a site that links to a site that I find offensive" challenge. An extreme example of this occurred with the IPL's Teen

Division, where we received some bad press from an Atlanta television news program because an AIDS prevention site in the collection linked to a site that linked to a site that linked to a site that linked to a site that had an obviously forged photograph of a naked Ellen DeGeneres. In the face of such challenges, your best tactic is to educate the challenger about the nature of the Internet and how just about any site is within six mouse clicks of something potentially offensive. One of my favorite weapons in fighting these sorts of challenges is Andy Ihnakto's excellent "Web That Smut" column (*MacUser*, January 1996),[5] which is both humorous and informative.

Another interesting challenge is the "Don't link to my site!" challenge. We've never had one of these at the IPL, but I've heard of them occurring elsewhere. My take on these is: if you don't want people to link to your site, don't put it on the Internet. Seems simple, but some people don't seem to get it. Generally in these cases you'll be dealing with people who have no clue as to how the Internet works, so an attempt at education is probably your best approach.

THE FUTURE OF INTERNET COLLECTION DEVELOPMENT

Predicting the future can be a tricky and dangerous business. Don't believe me? Go back to the library literature of 1990 and see what people were saying then about the future of libraries and librarianship. But at the risk of looking foolish a few years down the road, here's what I see for the near future development of Internet collections.

Self-Cataloging Documents
Wouldn't it be nice if documents could catalog themselves? Let's face it, cataloging Internet resources individually is time consuming and expensive. Since we are making electronic surrogates for items which are themselves in digital form, why not have the creators of documents embed within the documents

metadata that can be read and understood by a cataloging system? Makes sense, right? I hate to be a downer here, but here's my carefully considered opinion: It's a crock.

Admittedly there are some very attractive proposals being floated around, such as the Dublin Core project, and on paper they look pretty good. However, the practical application of any of these proposals runs into two problems.

The first problem is one of compliance. Given the fact that the number of publishers on the Internet is potentially every person on the planet with Internet access, it will be very hard to find a carrot or a stick big enough to entice or force compliance from all but a small fraction of the information producers on the Internet. This may come as a shock, but as important as things like cataloging, bibliographic control, name authority, and the like are to us librarians and information professionals, the average person could not care less about such things. For most people, if their sites are indexed by an Internet-wide search engine, that's good enough. They won't care about cataloging. Sure, if the system were simple enough, people would use it. But if a system were indeed simple enough so that anyone could and would want to use it, would it be much good? Yes, there are people who do care about such things, but most of us get sucked into librarianship or a like information profession.

The second problem is one of data integrity. Even if you are able to get enough people to go along with your scheme, you run into two types of people who will be responsible for putting bad metadata into your system: the evil and the clueless. The evil person will intentionally misrepresent a site within the metadata, either for personal gain ("I want my commercial site for selling wind-up, fire-breathing ducks to show up every time someone searches for President Clinton.") or just for the sheer malicious joy of it all. In a world full of spammers and hackers, your "good on paper" system doesn't stand a chance. The clueless, while innocent in intent, are perhaps a greater danger than the evil ones. Think about the lowest common denominator of Internet resource developer: the people who think that

15 animated GIFs and multiple frames in a Web page are a good idea; do you really want these people choosing their own subject terms from LCSH? And who on earth is going to write the training materials? Let's face it, bad metadata are worse than no metadata.

This is not to discourage the fine folks who are working on metadata systems to stop their work. In fact, many of the proposed systems show promise for uses on a limited, professional scale. But I think people should stop deluding themselves into thinking that the Internet will someday catalog itself. Of course, I'll be pleasantly surprised if I'm wrong.

Smart, Integrated Databases

A lot of the steps involved in maintaining a collection are tedious; who wants to sit there and check links by hand for a collection with 20,000 items? It would be great if we had a database that was built specifically for Internet collection development, much the same as QRC was developed for handling an Internet-based reference service (see Chapter 5). In my fantasy world this database would have an intuitive graphical Web-based interface for data entry; built in, easily modifiable templates for the user interface; a scripting language that is powerful and makes sense; and would be able to perform complex search functions speedily, no matter the size of the collection. In addition, this database would be able to assist (note: not take over) the maintenance functions. It could automatically check links during slow times and flag potential problem items to be brought to the attention of the librarian, freeing the librarian from having to check links one by one; but at the same time it would be much smarter about when links go bad and why. It could monitor certain areas on the Net (for example specific sections of the Yahoo What's New section, or designated Usenet groups), and identify potential items to be added to the collection. It could keep track of access statistics (the equivalent of "circulation") for individual items, letting the librarians know which individual items or areas of the collection are the most popular, or which resources are seldom if ever used and are candidates for weeding. It could pre-process patron suggestions, seeing if the suggestion is indeed valid, and checking whether the item is already in the collection.

Grand, Exalted, Distributed Collection Development

This leads me to my final vision for the future. At present, tons of Internet collection development projects are going on, from major undertakings like the IPL and UC Riverside's Infomine, to the individual projects in libraries throughout the world and personal pet projects all over the Web. Wouldn't it be great if we could all work together somehow? Much in the same way that the IPL is using librarians from around the Net to answer reference questions, we could also be signing up librarians to contribute to our collections. All we really need is Web-accessible database input and a good set of training documents.

Not that there should be just one main repository for Internet collections, as different people will have different approaches and different needs, but I foresee a world, and it's not too far off, with a dozen or so Internet collection projects, each with its own aim and focus, and its own group of people from around the globe to identify and catalog resources for the project. There could even be some sort of Internet Resource Approval Plan, where participating libraries could set up profiles with the big cataloging projects and have sub-collections custom built for their own patron base.

THE BIG, STAR-STUDDED CONCLUSION

Were this chapter a movie, at this point the hero would have the girl and the horse, and be riding off into the sunset. Alas, this is not a Hollywood Western, so you'll have to settle for a few words of encouragement.

You can do this. The skills and techniques and knowledge that you have developed throughout your career as a librarian are just as valid in the digital age, and in many cases even more so.

As a profession, we have been awaiting the promised information age. Now that it is finally here, let us seize the reins and journey forth boldly into a new tomorrow.

(Gee, it looks as though the hero gets the girl after all, or at least he gets the horse. Or perhaps it's a wind-up, fire-breathing duck. . . .)

NOTES

1. Controlled vs. uncontrolled: whether the terms come from a prescribed list or are made up as you go along.
2. One- vs. two-dimensional: whether the terms are applied individually, or can be strung together into a hierarchy. Multi-dimensional (faceted) systems are also possible.
3. The great science fiction author Theodore Sturgeon was once asked by a reporter, "Mr. Sturgeon, isn't it true that 90 percent of all science fiction is crap?" To which Sturgeon reportedly replied, "My good sir, 90 percent of *everything* is crap."
4. Traditionally known around the IPL as the "sucks/doesn't suck" test.
5. Andy Ihnnakto, "Web That Smut." *MacUser* 12, no. 1 (1996): 25–26.

Chapter 3

Creating a Successful Web Site

Schelle Simcox

CREATING A WEB SITE THAT KEEPS THEM COMING BACK

What makes some Web sites like the IPL successful at drawing people in and providing them with a sense of place, while other Web sites are less able to attract and maintain interest from visitors? Perhaps the IPL is a popular Internet site because it was created and adapted with a strong awareness of the library not only as "place" but as a place with specific values. Another reason may be because those of us creating the IPL kept sight of the primary goal of a Web site (and a library!)—to provide clear direction to content that people want, within a context that informs, educates, and leads them to deeper insight and investigation.

In a successful Web site, content, context, navigation, and place appear seamless. The Web site project manager knows that achieving this seamlessness is difficult, because it often requires careful planning and teamwork from many individuals with diverse skills, personalities, and expertise. In this chapter, I share the steps the IPL took each time we created a new resource for the library. The steps begin with identifying a potential resource topic, and move on to surveying financial, intellectual, technical, and structural issues. Next, the steps cover the development of a realistic timeline, and end with the unveiling, publicity, and maintenance of the new site.

This chapter is all about creating, designing, and maintaining special Web resources—those created from scratch or those created to display existing content in a new way. The focus here is on creating "original" or "adaptive" resources. Original sites are original. They are new creations, composed around a main subject, metaphor, or theme, using original content, rich context, and multiple avenues of access to a topic. Adaptive sites adapt already existing content, such as a reference work or a text, and take advantage of the Web as a dynamic publication medium.

The previous chapter deals specifically with the creation of "collections" of Internet sites. Although original and adapted resources have many similarities to a collection, they are entities in and of themselves, cumulating knowledge about a subject or theme. A collection of Internet resources does not focus exclusively on creating a sense of place; rather comprehensiveness and organization are the predominant considerations. For collections of resources, access is critical, but creating context is usually less of a focus. Perhaps the main distinction between a collection and an original or adaptive resource is that a resource succeeds in supplying comprehensive information on a specific topic.

Our resource creation process was informed and guided by our Ready Reference collection policy crafted early in 1995:

> The IPL will seek to collect Internet resources which:
> - Are high in useful content, preferably those *which provide information in their own right* rather than simply providing pathways to information
> - Are *updated consistently* (unless the nature of the resource is such that updating is unnecessary, e.g. an online Bible)
> - Are designed such that any *graphics are an attractive complement to the information* rather than a flashy distraction from it

- Provide text-only interfaces for non-graphical browsers (*develop for the lowest-common-denominator*)
- Show *evidence of having been proofread carefully* (no spelling/grammatical errors or faulty tagging)
- Contain only "live" *links, only to documents which are as relevant as the primary document*
- A resource which does not meet all the above criteria may still be added to the Ready Reference Collection if the selector feels that it is *still a useful source.*

As you can see, these criteria led us toward creating well-organized, timely, and tightly focused resources. These criteria form the basic philosophy that guided our creation or adaptation of new IPL Web resources. This selection policy acted as a strict quality guide, and forced us to select and create only those resources that added useful intellectual content to the Web.

ORIGINAL RESOURCES

One way to add content to the Web is to create an *original* resource. An original resource brings together all kinds of media (images, sounds, movies, animation, and text) on a specific topic or theme. This arrangement of media requires multiple avenues of access and an emphasis on good organization and design. The purpose of this resource is to inform, educate, and provide a full range of experiences on a topic. The Web offers an environment where all media can be experienced and new relationships can be created between previously unrelated material.

IPL's original collections were created either because an individual was particularly passionate about an idea or because we had a need for content not freely available on the Web.

POTUS: Presidents of the United States (see pages 90–92) is a good example of an original resource created because of one individual's expertise and passionate interest in a topic. In this case, Bob Summers had an interest in presidential history that was the basis for an award-winning IPL resource on the United

Lessons from a Seasoned Webmaster
Inside POTUS: Presidents of the United States

Imagining POTUS

Bob Summers created the Web site POTUS: Presidents of the United States in part because, at the time he was involved with the IPL, no sites on the Internet provided comprehensive information on all of the American presidents. Bob decided to focus his energies on creating his own Web reference resource on the American presidents. To create POTUS, Bob researched and compiled facts on each president, designed the content pages, then added links to historical media and related Web sites. "Providing annotated links is important in order to take full advantage of what the Web has to offer, although the inclusion of other Web resources creates a large maintenance issue."

One of the features that makes this resource stand out is the historical documents and primary source material linked to events listed in Presidency Highlights. Early in the design stage, Bob had a vague idea of how much content he would create for each president, but had no idea that his straightforward plan would become so complex with links to documents, video, and sound files. As his pages became complex and difficult to navigate, he began adding additional indexing and navigational features, so that visitors could understand the organization of the site at a glance. Focusing on navigation "allowed for easy access to each section of a page while letting the visitor know that there is a consistent structure to the site."

One valuable lesson he learned is that "If you create a resource, be prepared to answer lots of questions! People will consider you an expert and *will* send you e-mail." The quantity of e-mail Bob received once his site was on the Web came as a shock. "Having a Web site with any kind of 'mailto' tag encourages feedback, and I get five to ten e-mail messages a week. Some people send suggestions of sites to add, some ask for the collection development policy, and others suggest ideas for site design and praise or criticize the site." Any presidential scandal, anniversary date, or election also increases the visits and e-mail to his site. He maintains a current list of answers to Frequently Asked Questions and integrates them with the resource. This integration is an example of the kind of interactive content and community visitors bring to a Web site.

Fame and Fortune

In addition to many Web awards Bob has received, POTUS was featured in the *Seattle Times* on August 30, 1997, and was awarded the highest rating. He is particularly proud that the skillful organization of information was not only noticed, but applauded in the review. Authoring popular Web sites can open the door to other opportunities; Bob is currently writing a chapter for a Gale reference work, *Presidential Administration Profiles*, and *Atlantic Monthly* referenced his site in an article on the origin and recent use of the word "POTUS."

Audience

Many people want to know the primary audience of POTUS. His answer? "I designed it for myself." In creating POTUS, Bob wanted to create something that he would enjoy using. As a result of this focus, the site appeals to all age levels and interests. He has received e-mail from a mother who read the Truman page with her six-year-old son, reporters using the resource as a reference, and teachers requesting permission to use the resource in their classes. This last audience is the one that gives Bob the most satisfaction; it is particularly gratifying for him that a resource he created for his own interest and amusement appeals to and educates a new generation.

Lessons Learned

One of the important things Bob learned from the IPL was to "avoid creating Web sites that link to laundry lists of links" when creating a resource. "There is nothing more frustrating than to find a link on your topic that is simply a long list of more links. New resources should add value and original content to the Net. People can use search engines to find specific information; lists of lists overwhelm search results and provide little benefit. "A thorough and detailed resource answers the real needs of the Internet researcher. It is more important to add unique content to the Web. Find out what is unique in your community, region, library, or collection, and focus on that."

A Final Caution

"Don't create a resource that has already been done better than you could create. If you are creating a resource about the United States, make sure that you provide information on all of the states. Link or add content to an already created resource such as the IPL's Stately Knowledge instead of reinventing the wheel! Think about the information your audience wants to know."

Today Bob works at YachtWorld.com. He finds himself relying on his information science background and lessons he learned at the IPL. As an example, he tells the story of how a major corporation recently wanted to pay a large sum of money to create a full-page ad. This ad was designed to appear when the user clicked on the search engine from the home page. Bob had what he describes as a "librarian attack" in response to this proposal. "Easy access to information is key, and this ad would have been a barrier to that information in every sense of the word! The point is to organize sites so that people can find what they are looking for without burying the information under useless gimmicks or extra pages." He convinced everyone that it was not in their best interest to provide this type of advertisement and lose potential customers.

He has found that, although he now does programming and development for Yacht World, he has a different approach from Web developers who are not librarians. He finds that his colleagues want to develop the most technologically impressive, "bigger, better, brighter, flashier, site— to BLOW PEOPLE'S SOCKS OFF!" Bob's perspective is to "make sure that the technology does not get in the way of the information people are trying to find. Our Web visitors want facts, numbers, entertainment, information! For them, technology is not entertaining when it gets in the way. The way to get people interested in a product is to get them straight to the information they want. Keep this in mind when you create your resource. Large, animated images may be cool, but they take a long time to load. People may not wait for the image, and will leave without the information they sought."

Bob applied the same philosophy to POTUS. Technology should add value to the site. "Sound files were included so that people could hear the conviction in their president's voice, and video clips were included so people could see history when the president waves farewell as he boards his plane in disgrace."

States presidents. Bob created this resource to take advantage of his interest and to explore the possibilities in creating a resource on and for the Web. POTUS takes advantage of the Web's marriage of hypertext and multimedia and the application of a large database of content to create a rich, multilayered experience.

Whether a resource was developed because of a passionate interest on the part of the creator, or because the IPL was filling a need, creating original resources became one of the most creative and satisfying expressions of our work as librarians. The resulting stories, exhibits, educational resources, and reference collections added to our understanding of the Web environment. Creating these resources also underscored the importance of putting the user first, identifying access points and creating new pathways as necessary, organizing and evaluating information, locating relevant and important information, and understanding the information landscape and translating that for a visitor. One way we defined "access" on the Web was by interface design. While this is not a traditional library area of expertise, we became quite interested in creating interface designs that were easy for people of all ages and experience to navigate. Layout, organization of information, cataloging, and subject access became hot issues of debate and innovation, databases were created, new retrieval and access mechanisms considered, and meta-language issues became increasingly relevant in this environment. On the Web, in addition to providing e-mail reference service, "doing reference" also meant providing adequate pointers and pathfinders to related information and issues, and beginning to explore how to provide multiple kinds of services for the virtual library patron.

ADAPTATIONS

Another kind of resource we found ourselves creating at the IPL is an *adaptation*. In an adaptation much of the content is created and digitized based on a body of physical or intellectual content already existing in another format. In adapting a resource to the Web, we found that the transformation process always seemed to call for the addition of related content in a variety of formats in order to create the best possible resource. Libraries, archives, museums, associations, and individuals who possess documents, images, texts, and other media have begun to realize that the Web is a particularly appropriate medium to make their collections available to a new audience in new ways.

For the IPL, the Exhibit Hall and the Youth Division became the primary vehicles for creating original and adaptive resources.

The creative environment of the IPL made it easy for us to experiment and see what could happen when a variety of disciplines and traditions were brought together. During its first few years, the IPL allowed us to create new traditions of library service, based on traditional practices but with new outlooks and a wider variety of experiences to draw upon.

THE EXHIBITION AS A WEB RESOURCE

In early 1995 it became clear to IPL creators with archival and museum backgrounds that the Web had the potential to display collections in new ways. Early on, the Web showed potential as a vehicle for museums and archives to reach more patrons; they could use the Web as a form of outreach and publicity. More mileage could be gotten from valuable content by repackaging it via new formats for new audiences.

At the IPL, we began to call some of these original and adapted resources exhibits, because it was a metaphor that seemed to fit some of the resources we were creating and because libraries have a long tradition of exhibiting special collections. In creating an exhibition, we developed a themed resource, sometimes with an accompanying "catalog" or "tour," often with extensive collection notes or additional content notes. The exhibit metaphor works for many of these resources because of the nature of the Web. A Web exhibition could be any display of items that have a real-world physical counterpart, of a special collection of multimedia content, of a "reference" resource that deals with a specific topic in detail, or of any kind of Web page distinguished by a specific theme and scope. (See pages 95–97.)

The Key to a Block Buster Exhibit Hall

Online exhibitions have come a long way. Since the early 1990s, the exhibition of digital art on the World Wide Web has evolved tremendously in its design, scope, and conceptual sophistication. The first online exhibitions presented by museums, libraries, and other cultural content providers tended to offer a sampling of digital images from current exhibitions or permanent collections. These images were intended to showcase key pieces and entice the public to visit those institutions that housed the original artworks. In short order, content providers began to mount virtual exhibitions that precisely paralleled their counterpart physical installations. The design of these exhibitions employed the familiar metaphors of physical space: Web surfing visitors were welcomed into "main halls" and offered a selection of "rooms" or "galleries" in which to view the digital images on display. By the mid-1990s, much of this reliance on physical metaphors had diminished as content providers, representing institutions as well as individuals, explored new ways of using the Web as a design space in its own right. New virtual exhibitions appeared that could be seen nowhere but on the Web, having no counterpart on museum and gallery walls. Advances in the capacity of HTML to communicate form as well as function, while incorporating animation and multimedia elements, have further enhanced the sophistication of online exhibitions.

From its inception, the IPL was committed to providing space for exhibitions on its Web site. A small bunch of enthusiasts banded together to form the Exhibit Hall group, dedicated to the creation of interesting, entertaining, and educational online exhibitions for the IPL's diverse audience. Although these exhibitions were not strictly limited to art, all agreed that exhibitions were distinct in form and intent from other kinds of online resources. An online exhibition, as we defined it, is an ordered selection of images, text, sound, and other elements, all meaningfully linked by a coherent and unifying theme. In time, we developed guidelines and policies for the approval and development of exhibitions, the responsibilities of exhibition designers, the responsibilities of content providers, and the complex issues of intellectual property. Many online exhibitions have been mounted on the IPL site in its first three years, covering such wide-ranging topics as art, music, history, politics, and ancient cultures, to name a few. The Exhibit Hall is both perennially popular and critically acclaimed, and remains a tribute to the talent and dedication of the IPL's staff and volunteers, past and present.

—*Anna Noakes*

IPL Exhibit Hall: Roles and Responsibilities *
Draft: May 9, 1996
(with minor revisions: June 18, 1996)
Prepared by Anna Noakes

Exhibition Designer

- Conceptualizes and proposes exhibition idea to IPL staff for approval.
- Initiates and maintains contact with Content Provider(s) and Curator(s).
- Obtains agreement with Curator(s) on exhibition theme and content.
- Identifies stages of the project and sets internal deadlines for completion.
- Prepares the exhibition as follows:
    1. Obtains exhibition text from Curator(s).
    2. Edits and organizes exhibition text as required.
    3. Obtains all necessary credits for exhibition text (including credits for cited works, as needed).
    4. Obtains exhibition images from Curator(s) and/or Content Provider(s).
    5. Digitizes, sizes, color corrects, and stores exhibition images for photographic prints, negatives, slides, or color transparencies.
    6. Designs the exhibition layout, including the choice of fonts, sizes, colors, backgrounds, graphics, and other design features.
    7. Writes brief introductory text for top-level page of exhibition, describing the exhibition theme, Curator(s), Content Provider(s), and other details as needed.
    8. Writes short descriptive blurb for Exhibit Hall introduction page.
- Submits working version of exhibition to IPL staff and Curator(s) for review.
- Revises exhibition content and/or design as per review comments.
- Submits final version of exhibition to IPL staff to mount in Exhibit Hall.
- In conjunction with Curator(s), assists IPL staff to identify special target groups for publicity purposes.
- Informs Curator(s) and Content Provider(s) when exhibition has been displayed and publicized.

Curator

- Works with the Exhibition Designer to finalize exhibition theme and content.
- Selects images for exhibition and makes these available to Exhibition Designer.

- Writes and/or provides Exhibition Designer with exhibition text, including object data (descriptive information) for each of the images.
- Provides credits and any other information required to finalize exhibition text.
- Suggests order or sequence of exhibition images and text.
- Provides feedback on working version of exhibition.
- In conjunction with the Exhibition Designer, assists IPL staff to identify special target groups for publicity purposes.

Content Provider
- Approves collaboration of Curator(s) with the IPL and Exhibition Designer.
- Provides permission for IPL to use selected images and text in online exhibition.
- Ensures copyright clearance for all provided exhibition images and text.
- Establishes the chronological period (e.g., six months) during which time the exhibition may be displayed by the IPL.

Note

* Note that in some cases, an individual may occupy the roles of both exhibition designer and curator, and may even act as the content provider. These three roles and their respective responsibilities have been identified separately.

The effect of bringing together teams of talented people from a wide variety of disciplines was to create not only the Exhibit Hall but also an environment at the IPL where more sophisticated design and electronic information issues could be explored. Not only at the IPL, but elsewhere on the Web, new multifaceted "Web teams" developed innovative ways of providing access to information and organization and a new form of Web site began to appear on the Internet. These new resources incorporated an understanding of virtual space with active use of metaphor, employed sophisticated graphic and interface design, indexed and organized massive amounts of information, and developed ways to display multimedia and other technological innovations on the Web. How was this happening at the IPL and on the Web?

INTEGRATING MANY TRADITIONS

Creating the IPL from scratch and populating it with collections, resources, and exhibits within tight deadlines forced us to draw heavily on our varied experiences and expertise. Those of us involved with the IPL came from museums, archives, graphic and user interface design, computer science, and librarianship (including organization of information and cataloging, reference work, and public service). Some of us came from business, marketing, public relations, and newspapers. All of these areas of our expertise allowed us to explore the new Web environment while bringing many traditions to the new information technology.

One of the best things about the Web is the ability for the content developer to integrate many learning, viewing, and experiencing styles into the resource. No element in a resource sits in a vacuum; context must be created and integrated with the various forms of information and media. A resource in this genre links to other related sites in a collection and on the Web, pulls together experts and expert sites, and creates context. Usability is a large issue and new resources include pathfinders or finding aids to help guide the audience through a learning experience.

Maintaining a coherent theme and scope is a critical issue for this kind of information resource. So is the presence of human services and interaction. One issue we have come to feel strongly about is the importance of making our work as librarians visible to the library patron in the Web environment. At the Internet Public Library we take credit for our expertise in understanding the complexity of information organization and access, the information universe, and information-seeking behavior. At the IPL, we try to make it clear that human librarians created the library and the information resources. In light of the hundreds of messages the IPL receives each month, it is clear that the public recognizes and values human services and librarian expertise in the Web environment.

THE FIFTEEN STEPS TO CREATING A WEB RESOURCE

The following steps are an ideal checklist of tasks that I've learned through managing, assisting, or watching many projects take shape in the IPL. It may not be necessary or even useful to follow this list to the letter; however it is a pretty good overall guide to the kinds of decisions and issues that will come up during the development of any Web resource you create.

Step 1: Identify a Collection
Not everything should become a Web page. Many times, print or electronic resources already exist that do the job far better than a Web resource can attempt. You must ask yourself a series of hard questions before you commit your time, energy, and money to creating a quality resource. (And we assume you want to make sure it is a quality resource!) First and foremost, does this resource already exist? Has it been done before? Perhaps the resource exists in another format which you cannot hope to replicate. A perfect candidate for an adaptation is any unique

content that you (and only you?) possess and that can add intellectual value. If you are looking for fame and fortune on the Internet, find a *unique* collection that only you own, and that you are sure people will want to use once you adapt it for the Net.

Once you've located the unique idea or concept, what do you have to do to make this collection stand out? Is it possible to use local knowledge, archives, photographs, or expertise? Can you afford to be there to answer the subsequent queries from your new audience?

If you are convinced you have an idea for such a resource (or the most unique take on an idea), begin to survey your situation and resources and think about the following questions: What kinds of resources do you have? What physical attributes do the resources possess? If your unique resources are fragile letters written 100 years ago and they must be scanned, digitally indexed, or tagged with SGML, this process may take enormous care and money. However, the benefits may outweigh the costs if such a collection existing in electronic form will provide better access to the collection and added patronage for your institution. Perhaps your answers to these questions have only increased your interest in the possibilities.

"Decide what your collection will be about" (see Step 1 in Chapter 2) applies to the creation of any resource. First you must think carefully about your potential subject, scope, and audience. Deciding what your project will be about, like any aspect of the creative process, may go through many iterations as you work your way through the questions and steps. Once a decision is made and a team has begun the work of research and design, it should become clear that the original scope might have been too broad or narrow, and you must reexamine your original focus.

What should you create? Your resource should be *unique*, and there are many ways a resource can be developed to make sure that it is unique. It should probably be something that you are passionate or have special expertise about, or something that is central to your mission or collection. Every library, community, or organization has something unique (either historically, geographically, or in the form of personal expertise or content) that can and should be used as the core of a resource developed for the Web.

One might think that creating a Web resource would be simple. What could be so hard about putting together a few Web pages and images? It may be simple to begin a resource, but creating a quality, context-rich resource with adequate design and navigation can take enormous time and energy. A project can begin simply, but as the resource is developed, the complexity and time it takes to complete the project grows. Therefore, as in any work or exhibit, if you can narrow your original idea to one that you can adequately describe and excite people about in a few sentences, you are better off.

Any text that must be written, research that must be done, photos that must be scanned, graphics that must be created should be worked out in advance and a storyboard created in support of the final product.

Another question that should be considered in the brainstorming phase of the project is what formats of the source material will be used for your idea. Are there objects, texts, photographs, or other memorabilia that can and should be included in your resource and which will be needed in electronic form? What kinds of access should you provide for these items? Do you know what kind of display or layout will be required by the content holder? Have you received permission to copy and exhibit the originals in electronic form?

Step 2: Survey Your Resources

The next step once you have decided upon a theme, is to survey the resources at your disposal. How much money and time will this project take? The more expertise you possess, and the more time you can afford the project, the better your use of time and money. Do you have enough people with the necessary expertise to begin? What equipment will you need in order to carry out your idea? After an honest and healthy survey, what resources are you missing? It may be that at this point, you must redefine your expectations and ask yourself once again, "Can I afford this?"

Step 3: Do What You Can Afford—Create a Budget

A Web project budget differs in a few important ways from a typical budget. There is a high probability that outside expertise may be needed at some point in the process. The transformation or production of physical objects (such as photographs and digital images, or archiving) needs to be budgeted, along with storage costs associated with the digital maintenance of these objects. You may have to assess carefully or obtain bids for special technology or equipment. Often it is also crucial for the resource to receive a high level of publicity in the beginning, and this cost and expertise must also be budgeted into the project.

What is the long-term life of this project? Unless you specifically design a resource to require a minimum of upkeep, any budget for a Web resource must contain a category for ongoing maintenance and upkeep. Maintenance ends up being the biggest surprise in the budget of a Web resource. Many collections can be created so that they are static; that is, a decision is made to create a site with no links to outside resources. For the IPL, pictorial collections such as our Anarchist Images exhibit (www.ipl.org/exhibit/Labadie/) and the Pueblo Pottery exhibit (www.ipl.org/exhibit/pottery/) were both created with a minimum of maintenance features. All links to information are internal and there are no outside links to maintain. The mailto feedback tag is to the main library feedback pool, so there is no added maintenance. Any maintenance or interaction in the form of feedback or reference questions should be part of the equation when you calculate the budget. At the IPL, we quickly learned that any time we decided to create a new collection or exhibit, we needed to anticipate the maintenance costs.

Step 4: Assess Your Skill Sets (Or Recognize the Need for Outside Expertise)

Rarely does one organization or one person possess all of the skills needed to create a quality Web resource. Partnerships or outside expertise may be needed. Rule number one: Hire expertise but don't abdicate responsibility. As the originator of the project, you are the leader; you understand the overall concept and should be the driving force behind making sure that everyone is working toward a shared goal. The project manager must be able to explain or recognize technological or design expertise that would contribute a unique look and feel to the resource. The project manager should also have a clear idea of the final goal, but be flexible in approach and open to innovative ideas and solutions.

Technology folk, system administrators, and programmers all have their own ideas of what a Web resource should look like and how it should be created. It is crucial that education take place on both sides, but, from an information science viewpoint, it should be clear that usability is one of the most important considerations. Access points, retrieval, navigation, user needs, and user interface design must do battle with the latest flashy technology, inscrutable interfaces and design, or any of the latest technologies that are obstructive rather than accessible.

Designers too must be informed of the considerations and criteria important to your potential user community. It is critical to explain bandwidth and audience considerations to anyone designing graphics and multimedia. If you have to do too much explaining in the face of unhappy design ideas, perhaps the designers don't have enough Web expertise!

Web resources should stand up to traditional Web evaluation criteria. A resource should be evaluated on its authority, accuracy, objectivity, currency, scope, and format. The evaluation criteria you use to evaluate your own resource should be stated clearly to all participants during the design and construction phase of the project. Many times, finding a "good enough" solution and making creative use of the talents you possess are really all you need for a successful project.

Step 5: Consider Partnerships

It could be that resources are unique, but partnerships must often be developed with neighbor institutions to share the expenses of creating and maintaining your Web collection. Are the materials you plan to use for your research located internally or externally? If you own or have local access to the material, the issues you must consider are different from those if a special collection of material is located at a partner's location. Can local expertise be devoted to making your information special? Whatever added headaches result from a partnership, never underestimate the usefulness of capturing local knowledge to share with a worldwide community.

There are benefits of partnering with other organizations in your community. Building a Web resource is a good way to give something back to the community. Creating a resource in partnership with others can strengthen the library and community ties. The combination of partner expertise and resources will create better quality, and the publicity surrounding the project will build community for a long time to come.

With all of the benefits, why not work with multiple partners to create resources? Partnering with additional content owners does increase the potential for missed deadlines and other production headaches. Additional stakeholders add complexity and development time to the resource. Individuals must work harder to maintain good relations and make sure that all parties contribute fairly and are ultimately happy with the end product.

Some additional questions may arise in partnerships:

- Who will host the material?
- What are your partner's copyright requirements?
- What are the timeline requirements on their end?
- What skill sets will they be able to offer and how will you allocate responsibility?

- Who will be responsible for the maintenance of the material after the resource is unveiled?
- What financial resources do they bring to the partnership?

If the potential partner is not a library, you may find yourself needing to explain the work of the librarian to a partner. Much of what librarians do is not immediately obvious to your partners. What are the skills librarians bring to a Web project? For the IPL, we have found that we are especially expert in the areas of content, organization, indexing, navigation, access, user needs, knowing the information field, applying quality standards to resources (and how to evaluate them), interviewing, researching, and providing intellectual context for the potential audience.

It is important to stress to partners that providing adequate access to content may mean that search-and-retrieval mechanisms must be one of the highest priorities. The intended audience may need assistance in constructing appropriate searches or finding their way to the information they need. Ultimately, a resource is only as good as the avenues of access to its content.

Step 6: Build a Team (or a One-Person Show)
Four fundamental areas of expertise are necessary for resource development on the Web: artistic vision and design expertise, technological and programming expertise, content expertise, and organization and access expertise. It is possible for one person to be an expert in all of these areas, but more often, teams must be created. One caveat however: the larger the team, the more time you must allow for completion of the project.

Because the Web is a visual medium, graphic design and interface design skills are of critical importance. No site can overcome bad organization and design. Hypertext demands clear layout and navigation. The designer must understand how color, text, and white space work together to provide information to the user. The design must be flexible because Web resources change and revisions are frequent. An excellent design template can shorten the production time for everyone involved in a project. A designer should be willing and able to collaborate with the team in developing the design and providing important contextual design elements.

Complex resources may require extensive programming skills or system expertise. Some large resources require a database that is searchable and can output to the Web. Interactive sites require a programmer experienced with Web site architecture and design support. Early in our experience at the IPL, Nigel Kerr, our system administrator, made us create a wish list of things we wanted to achieve on our site whether or not we thought they were possible. Once we freed ourselves to brainstorm, many times we were able to come up with a creative solution that would not have been possible if we limited ourselves to what we thought was possible. Likewise, once the programmer or systems person has come up with a solution, it is important to work with him or her to test the interface with your potential audience and then make any necessary revisions. Often it is very difficult for a programmer or developer to understand how others will actually use the solution. Testing and revising are critically important.

Content expertise is a critical element of the team. The expert may need to author text and add research, or bring together additional media or text for a site. In most cases, the content expert should probably be the project leader or guiding force. In the context of information resources, content is king.

A person who understands organization and access of information on the Web is of critical importance for the creation of a usable information resource. Hand in hand with the technology, content, and design, understanding user needs and access issues is of paramount importance. If a site does not have depth and multiple access points, visitors may become frustrated and quickly lost in the Web environment. In many of the exhibits or resources in the IPL, we designed multiple ways to explore or experience a site.

This flexibility of multiple avenues of access is an obvious benefit of the hypertext medium. People should be able to find their way around the resource in many different ways and from many angles. This access may take the form of a search engine, along with a table of contents and a set of textual or visual navigation aids (arrows, hypertext links, maps, and so on), or traditional access points (such as author, title, and subject).

Each of the expertise areas (design, technology, content, and access), must communicate extensively throughout the development of the resource. Content, design, and technological support are often mutually driven and informed. A team that shares each draft and ideas at frequent intervals is a team that will probably create a critically acclaimed resource.

Step 7: Identify Technological Needs

Identify technological needs based on your subject and collection needs. It is difficult to keep pace with advances in current technology, so delay the purchase of software for your project until you are ready to use it. Survey available software and hardware for your project right before you begin, in order to find the best tools for your project for the best price. Develop a list of equipment necessary for your project. At minimum, software programs to manipulate images (such as Adobe Photoshop), Web page creation and design software, a scanner, and a server that can store large image collections are necessary. Designers may need special graphics software and image production hardware. If the project encompasses the creation of electronic text collections, sophisticated optical character recognition (OCR) software, hardware, and programming expertise will be needed. In addition to high-end software and production hardware, you will need servers with sufficient space to hold the collection and high-speed Web connectivity.

What kind of visual access should be offered for your collection? Some exhibits or resources necessitate the creation of large image files and electronic storage needs. If images are created, what size should images be, and what software should you use to create the images so that they are accessible via the Web?

If you plan to use materials from archives and special collections, careful handling and preservation considerations may be an issue. Electronic versions of archival materials are often a mandated solution in order to decrease the handling of rare and fragile materials.

Do you need a database? (See Chapter 2 for some issues to consider when creating your resource.) How important will search features be to your audience? Will you have extensive resources that may require complicated hierarchies or maintenance? In large, complicated resources, creating a database and managing your Web site with output from carefully designed and maintained databases may be the only realistic way to keep on top of your site.

Do you need programmers or system administrators? That probably depends on the complexity of your site. Supportive and knowledgeable programmers or systems folk can be a tremendous boon to your project and your sanity. Your technology support should be included in early budget planning and initial design meetings.

Once the site architecture decisions are made, make sure that everyone has access to the appropriate directories on your server. Plan a system and a methodology for monitoring updates and build the internal directories and subdirectories based on your site map or storyboard.

Web sites also require a variety of programming services which may be hard to predict early in the design of a site. Most sites will use scripts for forms, database search-and-retrieval, and other interactive service points. After the team outlines the content and defines the level of service that falls within your budget, it should be easy to group the kinds of programming needs and work with a designer and programmer to create the interactive elements.

Familiarity with Perl, Java, CGI scripting, and database output for the Web are critical skills to have on your team. (See Chapter 2 for a description of the kinds of scripts and IPL's results with CGI scripts and databases.) Most information-rich sites that lend themselves to search queries (that is, text-rich resources) can be improved by creating a database and designing the layout of your output to match your design template. This is one straightforward way to create a usable and accessible site. Currently, most basic forms and searches can be completed with rudimentary Perl or CGI scripting run against database output. There are many books that discuss creating an interactive Web site using databases and Perl, CGI, or Java scripts. If you are designing resources for the "lowest common denominator," you may want to limit the use of new Web technologies in your resource. Some applications may not be ideal for your resources. Much of the potential audience may not have the newest browser versions which can handle new technological improvements. Many current home and library users still have older browsers and slower connections.

Step 8: Identify a Basic Structure and Purpose
The first order of business is to get the team working together by identifying a basic vision and purpose. The team leader must be able to express the purpose of the resource succinctly and clearly to all members of the team. Keep a good record of the discussions and decisions the team makes, as many of the considerations developed by the team will become a part of the final "collection policy" or a section in the "About This Resource" area.

As the project progresses the team should be able to articulate the purpose of the resource, and this should serve to guide the team throughout the life of the project. In the end, a resource should always contain a section that states the purpose or policies related to the resource, authorship, contact and maintenance information, and the criteria your team used in creating content for your site. Usually, these policies or scope notes are in an "About This Resource" section of your site and should be placed in a prominent space on your site.

One of the critical steps in the development of a sense of place for a Web site is brainstorming the site's underlying architecture and layout. The designers should be informed by what you know about your users, how you imagine they will use your resource, and what they will do with the information they find. What should result from this brainstorming process is a diagram or tree-like structure outlining the major facets of your resource, major subject sublevels, and third-level subdivisions. (We usually don't divide the site any deeper, because that creates barriers to access.) One way to think of this is as a flat representation of a multidimensional space that users will be exploring and searching. To the best of your ability, you should attempt to think of this as a real (although virtual) space.

What infrastructure or architecture will you design for your site? The larger the site, the more important it is to design for growth and organization from the beginning. The layout of the site by the Web designers/architects should be developed in concert with clear communications with the systems or Web administrator. Develop a clear site map or hierarchical tree of the site layout on large sheets of paper or white board. (Paper is easier because you can save it and post it on the wall.)

Create storyboards or draw hierarchical trees representing the layout and navigation of the site. Keep these sketches current, redraw them as your understanding of your site architecture develops and changes. Name directory levels meaningfully, and make sure that the entire team understands the naming conventions and underlying structure.

A site tree will lead to navigation consideration. How will people move through your site? How can you accommodate their needs and design for optimum use? A rule that we used successfully is to design a resource that brings the user to the information they need in three screens or less. If you can manage it, never force someone down more than three levels of hierarchy before they get to the information they need. People rarely have the patience to plow through screen after screen—and if they are on the wrong path, multiple levels can be exceedingly frustrating.

A sense of place is also created by offering as many access points to the information as possible. Never underestimate the ways in which people may want to search for information or experience your site. The more paths to the content of your site the better. Often, though not always, offering many paths is easier to do by utilizing database output and search capabilities. In some cases, this can be achieved by cross-indexing your content in creative ways. Navigation and access work hand in hand to create a sense of place.

Another important aspect in identifying a basic structure is developing templates of your internal "record" or "content" pages. A template based on the design considerations and navigation should be planned and available to the team early in the process. Most likely, this template and design will go through many iterations as the site is tested and restructured.

The job of the designer is to work toward a consistent and unique look and feel for your site. It is the job of the rest of the team to remain true to the design templates and the agreed-upon structure. As developers discover important design changes to improve the look and feel and the navigation or structure of the site, it will be the job of the leader to maintain current template and design documents to reflect the desired sense of place—but to remain open to necessary design improvements.

It has been mentioned before, but it cannot be stressed enough, creating a sense of place is a mixture of understanding your audience and knowing your resource. Reflecting the intended purpose of the resource and information in design is one of the roads to getting to that nebulous sense of place that we feel is so critical for a successful Web resource.

Step 9: Identify a Style
We attribute some of the extraordinary popularity of the IPL to our ability to find a metaphor that worked for us and our patrons in the Web environment. I always knew that the small things—choosing a specific color, a unique font, and logo represented by a set of guiding principles in our "design dicta" (www.ipl.org:2000/backroom/training/DesignDicta.html)—were absolutely vital to our success.

The look and feel of a site should remain consistent and clean. However, after you have had a successful design and template for a while, it is a struggle to know when to stay with a winning design, and when to go for a fresh look. We witnessed all too many Web sites that developed a New! Look! only to discover that the improvements made the resource inaccessible and dismayed loyal patrons. Knowing when and how to redesign content is a delicate business.

Developing a theme or atmosphere is one of the most difficult and critical elements of a successful Web project or collection. Develop clear design criteria. How do you accomplish this? Does your organization already have a design style? Try to capture this style in your design. Check your brochures, your signage, your logo, your color theme, your physical or local architecture, furniture, or environment. Any identity or individual features of your physical environment can and perhaps should be carried over into a Web exhibit or collection! Much of this design work is achieved by working with a good graphic designer and developing and using a successful design template.

Step 10: Create a Design Template (Structure Encourages Creativity)

The IPL manages to work with hundreds of new students, teaching them how to develop resources that fit seamlessly within the IPL. One of the ways in which this is done is by sharing our design dicta and template (see Figure 3-1 for the IPL's design template) with each new member as an introduction to the IPL. It is clear from our experience that this structure produces creativity rather than stifling it as might be assumed. Likewise, your project should create a design template and design guidelines for each member of the team. The creation of a template is an iterative process. Rarely is the preliminary design successful enough to remain inviolate to the end of the project; the rough template may go through a few phases as the designer and the content develop a theme.

Templates go through approximately three phases. First, a

Figure 3-1. IPL Basic Template

```
<pre>
&lt;!DOCTYPE HTML PUBLIC "-//W3C//DTD HTML 3.2//EN"&gt;
&lt;html&gt;
&lt;head&gt;
&lt;title&gt;IPL Title of this Document&lt;/title&gt;
&lt;head&gt;
&lt;body bgcolor="#FFFFFF"&gt;

&lt;h3&gt;&lt;a href="/"&gt
&lt;img src="/images/ipl.logo.small.gif" alt="To the lobby of"&gt;&lt;/a&gt;
the Internet Public Library&lt;/h3&gt;

&lt;h1&gt;What This Is&lt;/h1&gt;
(Your stuff goes here.)

&lt;p&gt;&lt;stronger&gt;You may also wish to see &lt;/strong&gt;&lt;/p&gt;

&lt;p&gt;&lt;stronger&gt;Return to     &lt;a href="/"&gt;IPL
Lobby&lt;/a&gt;.&lt;/strong&gt;
&lt;hr&gt;

&lt;address&gt;the Internet Public Library - = - http://www.ipl.org/ - = -
ipl@ipl.org&lt;/address&gt;

Last updated
&lt;!—#config timefmt="%h %e, %Y"—&gt;
&lt;!—#flastmod virtual="this_file.html"—&gt;

&lt;/body&gt;
&lt;/html&gt;</pre>
```

draft template is created. As you begin to construct the site with content, a second template incorporates design elements and navigation. Finally, as the project draws closer to the end, the template is revised and all pages are brought in line with the final template.

Step 11: Refer to Dave's Steps

At this stage, if you find that you have a large collection of information and are thinking about incorporating it into the rest of your content, refer to the steps outlined in Chapter 2.

Step 12: Develop a Timeline and Beta Test Date

Establish an opening date and work backwards, identifying major project milestones and deadlines. It is important to include time to conduct a beta test and make revisions before the final opening date. Plan a beta test with users similar to your target audience. Groups designing and planning a site develop a terminology and understanding of the site which blinds them to alternative ways of thinking and planning. Watch your own interactions with first-time users. If you often find yourself justifying and explaining your methodology and design, then you probably have issues to resolve in your Web site design. Those working on the project simply cannot see the problems with their own designs—they are too close to the work. It is also very hard to take criticism of your own work. To test a design fairly, make sure that the person conducting the testing is not the person directly responsible for the content being tested.

When conducting user tests, ask questions but never explain and justify your design to the test subject. Tape or log user behavior and interview users after they have visited your site. Make sure your developers, technical folk, and designers review these tests. Seeing real people having trouble using your site is hard to disregard. You will always be surprised when your deliberate design to "make things easy" does not function as intended! Navigation is often one of the potential trouble spots. Make sure that every entry and exit point to content is clearly labeled and accessible. During the revision period, make changes to the site based on the user feedback. Try to look at your site as if you were seeing it for the first time. Does the site do what you intended? Take another page from the successful software designers book: take the time to conduct a user study.

Step 13: Create a Collection Development Policy

A collection policy answers critics and challenges to a collection. Challenges to the resource are easier to respond to when you have posted a clear and direct policy. When designing your site, your policy functions as a guidepost, keeping team members in focus. After opening and as time passes, collection policies are vital for helping future maintainers of your site understand how to expand the site, and understand your methodologies and focus.

At first, we were surprised by how often the IPL policies were referred to by visitors, ourselves, and students working on our site. Our audience, the patrons and visitors of our Web projects, asked questions, asked for justification, and challenged the contents often and in a variety of ways. The collection policy should include the criteria you decided upon for inclusion (exhibition theme and content) in the resource, your decisions about the scope and description of each item.

The experience of the Native American Authors (www.ipl.org/ref/native/policy.html) project was an important example of the importance of developing a collection development policy. As a liaison for the group developing this site, I stressed the critical importance of developing a collection policy. Because of the scope and content, the group members could easily anticipate challenges, by Native Americans and nonnatives, revolving around the definition of who is "officially" a Native American, and how we defined a Native American author. I advised the group to deal with this issue head-on, by working with native communities to define and build the resource, by carefully defining the scope and issues to consider. Once the site was open, the resource received questions and challenges about some of the material included in the resource. Because of this, they created a much more specific collection policy to respond to the challenges.

The collection development policy for a Web site becomes an important document for the life of the project. Once the project is completed, the policies or criteria associated with the design, inclusion, and scope must be publicly displayed on the site. As people begin to use the site, they may question the decision made for scope or inclusion. Just as in a print collection, a Web resource should have a clear description of the scope, purpose, and inclusion policy.

Step 14: Publicize the Web Site

Never underestimate the power of a good press release. Over and over, we have posted press releases to appropriate listservs to advertise our new resources and we were surprised with the results. Many libraries, reporters, and interested media representatives subscribe to these lists to keep up to date regarding interesting Web developments. A content or subject expert is another well-connected person who may be interested in disseminating information about the site to a wider audience. The IPL thus has mailed press releases to many people who may never check the standard online and print announcements for new Web sites. The IPL also has submitted new sites to subject indexers such as Yahoo, and other directories and search engines.

As a result of our publicity efforts, we have received many calls from radio personalities or journalists who wanted to interview us about our resource in concert with a show or newsworthy issue. In addition to seeking outside publicity, we advertise our new resources on our own site. Any publicity spotlights a new resource and can raise awareness of your organization's activities on the Web.

Step 15: Maintain the Site

Once you have created your site, and have begun to relax, you may notice something interesting happening. Suddenly it seems the entire world is sending you e-mail, discovering your library, and asking you questions! Not only that, but Web sites you have linked from your resource have changed location! You begin to realize that maintenance issues—keeping things current and adding newly created resources that match your collection, responding to users who write in to ask questions—may become a huge part of your job. It is critical to realize that this will be a result of your Web presence and to plan accordingly. If a high-maintenance site will not work in your situation or budget, make sure you take that into account and design a stand-alone site.

FINAL SUGGESTIONS

If you plan to create information resources on the Web, make sure to provide multiple layers of context. Frame the information with related resources and take advantage of the community of experts on the Web. Translate professional practices to the Web environment. There *is* a methodology for creating well-designed, complex informational resources that rely on traditional practices. Multimedia aspects of the Web provide people with ways to experience information in new ways. Improvements in Web design, browsers, and technology will continue to integrate sophisticated connections between people and information. Perhaps not too distantly, people will finally achieve Vannevar Bush's "memex" vision laid out in his July 1945 "As We May Think" *Atlantic Monthly* article.[1] People will create and archive their own information collections and experiences using a "seamless device" that stores "books, records and communication" as an "intimate supplement." As museums, libraries, and archives increase the output of their collections on the Web, there is a need for more sophisticated indexing and retrieval vocabularies and tools so that all people can find related information and content effortlessly. It seems that the realization of "access for all" moves farther and farther away as we add more and more information to the Web. National Archives projects and digital library efforts are increasingly emphasizing research into enhanced search and retrieval and a more sophisticated understanding of user behavior.[2] There is an increasing need to create information resources that add intellectual originality to our body of knowledge and take advantage of the movement toward integration of information. As POTUS's creator Bob Summers succinctly puts it, "Whatever you do, do it thoroughly." Or perhaps we should hark back to the clarity and focus that Charles Ammi Cutter outlined in his seminal work *Rules for a Dictionary Catalog*.[3] Although he was discussing the objects of a traditional print catalog, the words have resonance and are paraphrased here for a modern community. The object of our work on the Net should be to help users find the information they need, to show them what is available on a given subject, and to assist them in their choice of material. When I reflect on these core objects, I realize Cutter may have been a spiritual guide for the Web resource creation philosophy of the IPL from the beginning.

NOTES

1. Vannevar Bush. "As We May Think." *Atlantic Monthly* (July 1945): 101–108.
2. The Digital Library Initiative is sponsored by National Science Foundation (NSF), Defense Advanced Research Projects Agency (DARPA), Library of Congress (LC), National Library of Medicine (NLM), National Aeronautics & Space Administration (NASA), National Endowment for the Humanities (NEH), National Archives, and the Smithsonian Institution.
3. Charles Ammi Cutter. *Rules for a Dictionary Catalog*. 4th ed. Rewritten. (Washington, D.C.: Government Printing Office, 1904. Republished, London: The Library Association, 1953.)

Chapter 4

Serving Young People—
What You Can Do

Sara Ryan

The IPL's services for young people have attracted a considerable amount of positive attention since the library's beginning. In fact, the importance of youth services at the IPL has played a major role in my own professional development, as I shifted from the Reference Division to the Teen Division, and thus from academic reference to public library youth and young adult services, in the course of my time at the IPL.

In this chapter, I provide basic information about what kids expect from the electronic world and how they behave there, and present some of the issues that are raised when librarians create youth services for the digital realm. Then I use IPL projects to illustrate the processes you will need to go through when you create these kinds of services in your own library.

WHY CREATE INTERNET-BASED SERVICES FOR YOUNG PEOPLE?

This question may seem so basic as to be not even worth asking. It is obvious to most librarians that young people are a tremendously important component of any public library's patron base, and that public libraries have traditionally provided services for young people. It is also obvious that this tradition should not change with the introduction of the Internet into a library's collections and services.

But the question is worth asking and answering for the simple reason that librarians are increasingly expected to justify *all* of the services they provide. That justification may result in a greater number of staff being allotted to a particular project, newer equipment being purchased, or a grant being awarded. Or it may mean simply that the budget will not be cut as drastically as it would have been without the justification.

If, for example, you wish to have a youth librarian spend 20 percent of her time creating a youth-focused Web site, you will most likely need to come up with a more substantive reason for the expenditure of that time than "It's a good idea, and other libraries are doing it." From an administrator's point of view, this answer is simply not adequate to justify spending many hours of staff time to develop services that then may not be used by their intended audience. To find more persuasive answers to the question, it is useful to examine briefly how youth services have been justified in traditional public libraries.

Why has service to young people been an important part of the mission of public libraries for so long? The reasons range from the noble to the pragmatic. From a purely service-oriented standpoint, it is vital to introduce youth to library services as early as possible, to foster their intellectual and social development most effectively. And from the most pragmatic, bottom-line standpoint, every child is a future taxpayer. If young people are introduced to library services at an early age, they are far more likely to continue to use, value, and support the library as adults.

These reasons for including youth in public library mission statements translate fairly well into the digital environment. From the service perspective, kids need to develop the skills that comprise information literacy. They need to be able to navigate successfully among multiple media, and they need to be able to make educated decisions about what kind of information source best suits their needs for a particular project. Librarians make these kinds of decisions constantly, as we develop our collections and answer reference questions for our patrons. Librarians are therefore best suited to teach kids how to determine which topics can be researched the most productively using which kinds of information resources. However, there's no reason that the definition of library has to be limited to a building full of books, and there's no reason that librarians can't interact with kids digitally as well as in person.

From the pragmatic perspective, if we don't show kids what libraries have to offer, especially as our culture becomes more and more oriented toward instant information gratification, they won't understand what they're missing. They won't know what they don't know, and they won't support libraries when they're the ones paying the bills. Again, there is call for a more expansive definition of what a library is and what services librarians can provide.

WHAT SERVICES ARE APPROPRIATE?

One reason that creating Internet-based services for youth has not been a smooth and easy process for public librarians is that adding the Internet to the pool of resources offered to children and young adults raises many questions, both for librarians and for society as a whole. The most controversial question—and thus by far the most frequently discussed—is, of course, whether children and young adults should have open access to the Internet in public libraries. This question is treated later in the chapter.

But there are numerous other questions about what types of services are appropriate for librarians to provide to youth in this environment. The vast amount of attention being given to installing (or not installing) filtering software is preventing librarians from thinking about what happens *after* they decide what they're going to do technologically and philosophically.

I have provided the questions and scenarios below as a small sampling of the kinds of issues that the use of Internet technology raises. You might want to discuss these questions and scenarios in a meeting of your youth librarians, present them to your administrative staff to expand their awareness of these issues, or simply think about them on your own as you plan services or consider modifying the services you already offer. Remember, when considering these scenarios, to take into account staff time and expertise as well as financial and technological resources.

- What is the youngest age for which you would plan a program that includes use of the Internet? Why?
- Would you allow children to count Web sites as part of their summer reading? Would one screen be considered the equivalent of a page of printed text? Would you allow them to read commercial sites, or restrict them to educational sites?
- You have recently received, via a mailto link on your "Homework Help" Web page, a number of messages from kids who seem to be seeking personal counseling rather than homework information. How do you respond to these messages?
- You surveyed teenagers in your community to find out what they most wanted to learn about using the Internet, and the overwhelming majority answered, "Chat rooms." Do you provide training in how to access chat rooms? Why or why not?
- In the same situation as the previous question, how would your approach differ if the teenagers had answered, "Learning HTML and building our own Web pages"?
- Your library has traditionally hosted after-school homework help programs where volunteers assist youth with their assignments. Surveys have indicated that youth would like to be able to contact the homework help volunteers remotely via e-mail or in a text-based virtual reality environment such as a MUD (Multi-User Domain). A group of young adults has volunteered to do the initial programming to create a

MUD if the library will then maintain it and staff it with the homework help volunteers. Would you agree to the young adults' proposal? Why or why not?

- Your library's Web site offers patrons the option of sending in reference questions via e-mail. The reference staff responsible for answering the questions complain that many of the questions seem to come from children who cannot express their needs clearly. Staff recommend either that the service be discontinued or that patrons be required to input their ages when they send in questions, so that children's questions can be forwarded to the youth librarian. What course of action would you take?

- The youth advisory board at your library has been working for months on their own section for the library's Web site. They are particularly enthusiastic about the graphic design, and feel confident that the pages will draw some of their peers into the library who otherwise might never have darkened its doors. When you look at the pages, however, you realize that the group has pulled many of the graphics from other Web sites, without giving credit to the original designers. Do you ask the board to do a redesign? What other options do you have?

CHARACTERISTICS OF THE FIRST WIRED GENERATION

The kids who are growing up today are the first generation that accepts computers as a given, as a mundane, normal part of their daily lives. The kids who don't have computers in their homes have used them, or at least seen them, in schools or libraries. If they haven't been exposed to them in any other way, they've seen computers in movies or on television.

This means several things, all of which librarians who want to serve kids should keep in mind. Kids aren't scared of computers, or at the very least they aren't intimidated by them the way adults who haven't grown up with the technology are. Kids will push buttons and move the mouse around without worrying that they're going to break something—even if they're about to do so. They are also not easily defeated: if clicking on one part of the screen doesn't make anything happen, they'll click somewhere else.

Kids have higher expectations about what they can do with computers—and not necessarily only *higher* expectations than previous generations, but also simply *different* expectations. These expectations are different precisely because kids don't have the same sense of the limitations of this technology that adults have. Most adults, even if they have lost hours of their lives playing Doom or Myst or Tetris, still think of the computer primarily as a device that is intended for getting work done. Most kids, on the other hand, approach any new computer with the question "What games does it have?" Kids who have always thought of computers as machines that you *play* with will experience and interpret them in a very different way from an adult who has spent a long time painstakingly learning how to navigate within a Web browser.

Today's kids are required to use computers in school far more than any previous generation—not only to learn different programs, but also to use the Internet for research. However, there are varying interpretations, both by the kids and by their teachers, of what "using the Internet for research" actually means. A kid might decide that it means downloading her entire paper from www.schoolsucks.com.

And although kids aren't intimidated by computers, they are likely to be confused about the specific details of how they work: for instance, how a Web browser accesses Web sites, or the difference between the Internet and America Online. Software designers, as they attempt to integrate Web browsers, word processors, databases, spreadsheets, and even games into one uniform computing environment, are not helping to clarify this confusion. It is thus crucially important to remember that when a kid tells you that he knows "everything about the Internet," you and he may have very different definitions of "everything."

A recent book that discusses the characteristics of kids' relationship to computers in some length is Don Tapscott's *Growing Up Digital: The Rise of the Net Generation* (New York: McGraw-Hill, 1998). The book presents a very optimistic picture of the ways the world will change when the "Net Generation," as Tapscott calls them, take over the workforce, politics, and education. The book is valuable despite its rose-colored perspective because it provides several examples of the kinds of interaction and projects real youth have experienced and created in the Internet environment.

RESEARCH ABOUT KIDS AND COMPUTERS

The design of software for children has become an extremely profitable industry, and the study of how children respond to computers has become an active academic discipline. Scholars study the differences between the ways boys and girls use computers, track physiological responses to on-screen stimuli, and analyze the online personas kids (and adults) adopt in virtual reality environments. Game designers try to find the right blend of action, narration, music, and graphics necessary for a game to attract both genders—or abandon that problem and design specifically girl-oriented games, since the default audience for games is boys.

But it would be far beyond the scope of this book, let alone this chapter, to attempt an exhaustive review of current thought about kids' use of computers. I will recommend that readers interested in the research start with Sherry Turkle's *Life on the Screen: Identity in the Age of the Internet* (New York: Simon and Schuster, 1995) and Seymour Papert's *The Connected Family: Bridging the Digital Generation Gap* (Atlanta, Ga.: Longstreet Press, 1996). Turkle and Papert have both spent years examining the ways children (and adults) work and play with computers. Both authors provide detailed analyses of computer use by real kids, and both consider the psychological ramifications of computer use in some depth, with a particular focus on the ways computer use can change the ways kids learn.

However, reading about the ways kids use computers isn't enough. You will learn at least as much from watching kids as you will from reading a scholar's interpretation of their behavior, if not far more. Walk around your library and watch kids searching for information. Think about questions like these:

- Do they approach the search differently when they're using the online catalog from when they're using the Web?
- When do they give up the search, and why?
- When they're playing, just looking for stuff for fun, what is that process like?
- How does it differ from the way they search when they're looking for information for a school report?

The more you can observe, the better ideas you will have about how Internet-based services can work for your library's young people.

THE IPL'S APPROACH TO SERVING YOUNG PEOPLE

All the projects and services the IPL has developed for young people function as answers to the question "What happens to youth services when your library exists only as pixels on a screen?" There are obvious disadvantages to creating a story hour for kids whose faces you never see, or assembling a youth advisory board of teenagers from several different time zones. But the IPL's purely digital existence is not solely a disadvantage; it does require staff to implement creative and innovative strategies for serving youth. These strategies are outlined below in three sections, which describe services for children, services for teenagers, and the creation of substantial original content. Also discussed are the various sorts of e-mail feedback that creators of youth-oriented library Web sites are likely to receive, and how best to respond.

Services for Children

The IPL Youth Division began to take shape early in 1995. At that point in the Web's development, sites designed for children were conspicuous in their absence. We were still a long way away from the Communications Decency Act and the current controversy about filtering software and children's access to the Internet, not to mention the explosion of commercially oriented sites for kids. It's also worth mentioning that the group working on youth services, hereafter known as "the Youth Division" (the name refers to both the people who developed it and the Web pages of which it consists), was not made up of people with substantial technical backgrounds. Quite the contrary, most of the group's members were novices in the realms of writing HTML, creating and modifying graphics, and recording audio files. They knew what they wanted to do: write, illustrate, and tell stories; hold a writing contest for kids all over the Internet; get prominent authors and illustrators to respond to questions from children; demonstrate a science experiment; have an interactive book discussion group; and create a kid-friendly "space" where all these services could exist. They learned the necessary technologies as they went along, and also drew on the expertise of their liaisons from the Architecture group (see Chapter 1).

In 1995 when the Youth Services team, led by Josie Barnes Parker, made the decision to dedicate a section of the IPL to youth, they were also making a decision to create original content. They could not simply have put together a collection of sites for children, the way some librarians do in today's Web, because the sites weren't there. In order to provide any kind of service to kids at all, they were forced to become content providers. (However, they recognized that they would want to include links to other sites eventually; the Youth Division Selection Policy [see Figure 4-3 in this chapter] addresses that point.)

But the Youth Division could just as easily have chosen to design the division with a focus on parents, teachers, or youth librarians. The fact that they did not—that they *did* design the division with substantial original content intended to be used by children—is one of the reasons that the IPL received so much media attention so early on. This focus on kids, rather than on the adults who serve them, has also continued to influence the IPL's philosophy of youth services through the development of the Teen Division and of the magazine *WebINK: Internet Newsletter for Kids*, both of which are discussed in greater detail later in this chapter.

As Joe Janes points out in Chapter 1, the combination of services the Youth Division put together was an interesting mix of programming found in a traditional public library and new ideas that came from the Internet environment. Perhaps the most interesting challenge that the Youth Division faced, after they had determined the content they intended to provide, was how to create the "space" for the content—in other words, how to design a site for children.[1]

DEFYING THE DESIGN DICTA

The Youth Division was granted a blanket exemption from the IPL's design dicta, as mentioned in Chapter 1, because a kid-oriented space on the Web needed to look different, the same way the children's room in a public library looks different from the rest of the library. The division used a number of strategies to create kid-friendly pages; following are detailed descriptions and a discussion of how you can use these strategies on your kid-focused site.[2]

Large font size. Kids who haven't been reading for very long find it easier to read larger type, so it's good if at least the headings on your Web pages are in a large font. This can be tricky, because to some extent, fonts in a Web site are always at the mercy of the user. Jane Q. User can set her browser preferences so that all the Web pages she views appear in her favorite font, in her favorite size. However, there are a few ways to ensure that Jane will see your pages the way you want them to be viewed.

- Define a default font and font size in your HTML code. The way to do this is to use the <FONT FACE> tag. Here's an example of how that looks:

  <FONT FACE="Arial, Geneva, Helvetica" SIZE="+2">

  The reason for three different font names in the example is to accommodate different types of computers, because PCs and Macintoshes are typically loaded with different fonts.
- Use text-based graphics instead of all plain text. It's a bad idea to do this for an entire page of information; not only will the page take forever to load, it will also require you to use a vast number of <ALT> tags (tags that are used to describe graphics for people using text-only browsers and/ or screen readers). But if you want to make a striking, eye-catching heading, for example, try a text-based graphic. For an example of text-based graphics in action, check out the IPL's homepage at www.ipl.org.
- Use heading tags for your body text. People who are strict about using HTML to define a document's structure will frown on this usage, but it works. If you put a paragraph within an <H1> or <H2> tag, it will definitely be displayed on Jane's screen in a larger size than she would normally see text.

Graphics. Graphics are a big can of worms. It's very hard even for professional designers to create images that will show up attractively on all browsers and operating systems. But graphics are attractive to kids, and you will want to have them, at least in some quantity, on a site designed for kids. However you obtain your graphics, make sure you know how to compress them. You want your graphics to be as small as possible in terms of file size, because larger graphics mean that your users will have to wait longer for them to download. Here are some ideas for obtaining graphics for your kid-oriented Web site.

- Find a professional designer who's willing to do pro bono work in exchange for a nice credit on your Web site. Or find an amateur designer who wants to get more experience. Illustration and design classes at local universities, colleges, and community colleges are a good place to look for prospective designers.
- Buy a digital camera and take pictures of events and programs at your library. Use these images on your Web site. (Note: if your photos include pictures of kids, *always obtain permission from parents* before putting them up on your Web site.)
- Use free clip art. I'm not a big fan of most clip art, as you will definitely learn before the end of this chapter. But with careful searching, you can find some images that don't immediately say "clip art" to the viewer.
- Buy a scanner, or find someone who will let you use one, and have kids draw pictures that you then scan and put up on your site. Make sure to tell the kids to use bright colors and thick outlines when they draw.

Color. Entire books have been written about how to color Web graphics[3] and it's worth your while to check out at least one of them before you start putting your site together. It's also important to remember that some of your users are color-blind, and you don't want to use colors in combinations that a color-blind person can't perceive. (Some users will be blind, too, but you will accommodate them by using <ALT> tags and avoiding frame-based navigation, which does not work well with screen-reading programs.)

Large icons to click on in addition to text describing various options. Icons are easier for young children to identify and click on than an underlined word or sentence.

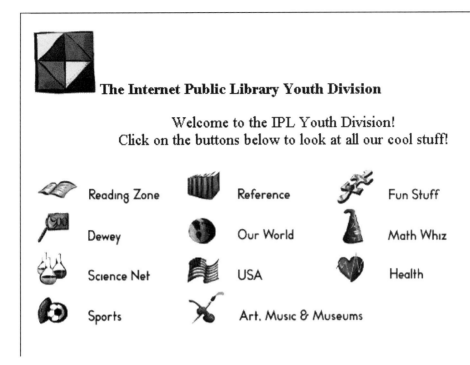

Figure 4-1. Current Youth Division Home Page.

Short sentences, simple word choices. Think about how you speak to kids when you're doing a storytime or answering their questions at the reference desk. Use the same kind of language on your Web site.

Though the design of the front page of the Youth Division has changed many times since the IPL's beginning, the same design strategies have been used consistently. Figures 4-1 and 4-2 illustrate IPL's use of these strategies.

While the Youth Division—and the rest of the initial version of the IPL—was in the process of being created, the idea of "getting it done" was paramount in everyone's mind: the goal was to finish the projects and put the Web pages out there for the rest of the world to see. It was apparent almost immediately, however, that on the Web, there's no such thing as "done."

FEEDBACK, MAINTENANCE, AND WEEDING

As we discovered in developing the IPL, there are certain characteristics shared by projects that thrive, as well as characteristics shared by the projects that do not grow.

To borrow a term from computer programming, the projects that thrive are *object-oriented*: that is, they consist of discrete "chunks" of information that can either stand alone or be combined with other chunks to make a larger whole.

For an example, consider one of the stories on the IPL Story Hour, "Molly Whuppie," created by Antoinette and Meaghan Murphy. You can choose simply to read the text of the story, a traditional English folktale. You can choose to read it and look at the illustrations. Or you can choose to read the words, view the illustrations, and hear the story narrated to you. Any one of these options could stand on its own perfectly adequately, but the fact that you can choose among them enhances the value of the project. It's true that "Molly Whuppie" is just one story. But it can be combined with other stories to make up the larger whole of the Story Hour, which is still an important part of the Youth Division—which in turn is a part of the overall IPL.

Another characteristic of projects that thrive, related to the notion of being object-oriented, is that they are *finite*. If you decide to make pages that illustrate the steps of a science experiment, when the experiment is done, so are you. You may choose to add more science experiments at a later date, but for the present, you have a finished product. This approach also allows for the Web site to grow in a planned, gradual fashion rather than in the haphazard, unrestrained way that can result in some parts of a site being spectacular and other sections being stale.

Projects that thrive are *well-defined* and have a definite *scope*. If it's difficult for you to figure out exactly what you want to do for kids on the Web, decide first what you *don't* want to do, and define what you *will* do based on that. For example, if you don't want to run an online book discussion group for kids, maybe you can decide to put up two or three booktalks each month instead.

Projects that don't thrive are not bad projects. For instance, the idea of having an interactive book discussion group for kids, led via e-mail, could probably be very successful.[4] It was problematic in the IPL, however, both because of the constant need for updating (choosing new books, posting topics for discussion, and so on) and because it was difficult to target and then retain a group of kids.

However, the idea of getting kids to comment about books that they have read remained an important one at the IPL. Mary Pat Timmons eventually created the very successful IPL project, A World Of Readers, which is a collection of book reviews by children. Individual kids could send in reviews, or teachers and librarians could coordinate whole classes to send in reviews. In A World Of Readers, kids were free to send in reviews of whatever books they wanted to. But you could also design a project wherein you feature different books each month and solicit reviews from kids. Again, this is a flexible, object-oriented approach to accumulating content.

Many of the projects, both in the Youth Division and elsewhere in the IPL, that have fallen away over time have done so because they required more frequent maintenance and updating than was possible given staff resources. The projects that have been the most successful have either been self-contained— each individual story in Story Hour, for instance—or designed with a structure that allows for continual growth without the need for simultaneous revision of preexisting material, such as A World of Readers or Ask the Author (now known as Author FAQs). There's no way for the children's book reviews to go "out of date," or for the authors' answers to children's questions suddenly to become inaccurate. But it's always possible for more children to send in book reviews, and it's always possible to solicit more authors to respond to children's questions.

A brief digression to treat the Ask the Author project in a bit more detail is appropriate here, because it illustrates some of the changes that began taking place in the culture of the Web during the first several months of the IPL's existence. When Josie Parker began to work on the Ask the Author project, she solicited the participation of authors and illustrators by postal mail. Very few authors and illustrators used e-mail at that time, and in fact some of the authors and illustrators did not own computers. By the time the project had been "live" for a while, however, authors and illustrators began to contact the IPL to request that they be included in the project—and they frequently made their requests by e-mail. Now almost all major publishers have Web sites that include author profiles and that give users at least a token opportunity to communicate with the authors via mailto links. Many authors also have personal Web sites.

Services For Teenagers[5]

As we discovered in the process of putting together the IPL Teen Division, making Web sites for teenagers is in some ways easier and in other ways more challenging than creating sites aimed at younger kids.

It's easier because:

- Teenagers are typically more accomplished readers than younger children, so you don't have to simplify your language so drastically.
- Teenagers have greater hand-eye coordination than younger children, so there is not as much need to use large icons in design.
- Teenagers are old enough to be articulate about what they actually *want* from a Web site, and you can ask them directly about what services they consider most important.
- There are lots of teenagers out there who are making sites, so you can actually link to sites designed by members of your target audience.

It's harder because:

- What teenagers want from a Web site may not be anything you feel qualified to provide (e.g., chat room access or the latest information about bands).

- As all program-planning young adult librarians know, just because you design something for them doesn't mean that teenagers will like it, use it, or provide any feedback to you about it (whereas with younger children, you'll get feedback from the parents if not from the kids themselves).
- Even if you get input from teenagers about the kinds of sites they like, you may not agree with their choices (more about this later on).
- The subjects that teenagers need and want information about are frequently controversial (sex, drugs, and rock and roll).

And then there's the other problem associated with making Web sites (or anything) for teenagers: the coolness factor.

THE "COOL" CONUNDRUM AND DESIGN FOR TEENAGERS

Everyone who wants to appeal to teenagers wants to be perceived as cool. It's a losing battle. Even if there were such a thing as a Platonic Ideal of Teenage Coolness, which there most decidedly is not—teenagers' taste is as diverse as adults'—the ideal would change before you could design a Web site that reflected it. Thus, it's not possible to define the characteristics of good site design for teenagers as you can for younger children. However, there are a few things that you should keep in mind when designing a site for teenagers.

- Be as graphically sophisticated as you possibly can. Remember that advertisers who have more money to spend on a single ad than you have in your entire year's budget are targeting these kids all the time. Note that "graphically sophisticated" does not mean making extensive use of the clip art collection that came with your PC. If your budget allows it, think about bringing in a professional designer. If it doesn't, at least spend some time looking at the commercial sites that are popular with teenagers, like the Gap's site (www.gap.com) or the NBA's (www.nba.com), and think about the strategies those sites use to get and keep viewers' attention.

- Use bells and whistles, but use them judiciously. I use the phrase "bells and whistles" to refer to page design using such elements as frames, Java, Javascripts, animated GIFs, streaming audio, streaming video, chat windows, or that evil plug-in that plays background music incessantly and that you can't turn off. Think about using some of these gimmicks on your pages, even if they drive you crazy. Pick the ones that annoy you the least; however, don't include so many that your pages cause your Web browser to crash, and don't design in such a way that your bells and whistles are integral to navigating your site. (For example, if you design a site using frames, provide a frameless version.)

- Use intuitive language. Stop thinking like a librarian. Think like a teenager. This is perhaps the hardest thing to get right. If you try too hard to be hip and current (for example, "Check out these dope and phat links to tight sites!") you run the risk of looking exactly like what you are: an adult trying desperately to ingratiate yourself with teenagers. On the other hand, if you veer too far off into the land of complicated subject headings and librarian jargon, you will also lose your audience.

But the most important thing to do when you're designing a site for teenagers is—surprise—to look at sites designed by teenagers! And as suggested above, look at the commercial sites that have a large teenage audience, such as MTV, Nintendo, band sites, and sports sites. This exercise will help you get a sense for the kinds of pages that look contemporary.

CONTENT FOR A TEEN-FOCUSED SITE
When we were first putting the IPL Teen Division together, we solicited feedback from the Ann Arbor District Library's Youth Advisory Board about what subjects they would be interested in having us cover. If you have a youth advisory board at your

library, ask them what they want to see! Another way to glean information about topics of interest to teenagers would be to post a questionnaire (in your library, on your Web site, or both), to which teens could respond with information about their interests and needs.

The initial version of the Teen Division balanced sections linking to sites containing information about serious issues with sections linking to sites treating more entertaining topics. The four initial sections of the division were Entertainment, Colleges and Universities, Social Services, and Sports. Because the Teen Division covered some of the same topics also addressed in the Ready Reference collection (Entertainment, for instance), the Teen Division focused on sites that had either been designed by teenagers or were specifically addressed to them. The Teen Division Selection Policy (see page 139) defined the criteria for selecting resources. Note that the policy directly mentions that some sites containing vital information for teenagers are by their nature controversial.

If you plan to make a site for teenagers that includes more than a few links to Web sites outside your library, we strongly recommend that you develop some kind of selection policy. It's almost a given that someone will challenge some aspect of your site, and it's far easier to deal with such challenges if you have a policy to which you can refer the complaining patron.

...searching and surfing...

Your suggestions and a real librarian select fun & useful sites from all over the Web.

Arts and Entertainment
Books and Writing
Career and College
Clubs and Organizations
Computers and Internet
Dating and Stuff
General Homework Help
Health
Issues and Conflicts

Teen Division Originals

Resources created right here at the IPL.

- Improve your research papers with the A Plus Research and Writing Guide.

- Figure out what to do with the rest of your life with Career Pathways.

- Check out our page in honor of Teen

Figure 4-2. Teen Division Home Page.

Figure 4-3. Teen Division Selection Policy.

IPL Teen Division Selection Policy
http://www.ipl.org/teen/selecpol.html

The Teen Division is guided by two broad selection policies, the Internet Public Library's Materials Reconsideration Policy and the Teen Division's Selection Policy described below.

Teen Division Policy
The collection of the Teen Division of the Internet Public Library is developed for teenagers ages 13–19 and their parents, teachers, and anyone else interested in information directed to and about teenagers and young adults. Material used and sites recommended are chosen based on their appropriateness for the subject matter and should be written and maintained by an authoritative source. The information should be current, accurate, and presented in an objective and well-organized manner. While the resources may not necessarily be aimed specifically at teens, their contents should be of interest and useful to these age groups.

Some areas of the Teen Division cover information about difficult topics with which teens are confronted in today's rapidly changing society. The teen years are a time of tremendous growth and development, and today's teens are exposed to issues and experiences that would challenge even adults with the most developed coping skills. The Internet is potentially one such source of exposure for teens, yet it also has profound potential for information dissemination that teens desperately need.

The IPL Teen Division seeks to provide teens with access to basic information about many of the difficult issues they face. In doing so, we recognize that we have provided links to sites which some teens and adults will consider inappropriate. We actively seek sites that are authoritative and we avoid sensationalistic sites that lack content. At times, however, we make the decision to include sites that have potentially questionable material because the usefulness of other information at the site makes that site's benefits outweigh its disadvantages.

The IPL Teen Division strongly encourages teens and parents to participate in open dialogue whenever possible. We recommend that parents explore the Internet and establish appropriate rules for use with their teens. We recommend that teens discuss their experiences on the Internet with a parent or trusted adult, especially when that exploration results in viewing sites that contain information or images they find confusing or disturbing.

E-Mail and Its Malcontents

Because of the nature of the IPL, e-mail is the only type of feedback we receive from the majority of our patrons. This fact makes for particular challenges when the patrons are young people who may be confused about the purpose of the site or about exactly what services the Youth and Teen Divisions provide. (That is not to suggest that adults always find it easy to navigate Web sites or to understand the purposes of sites.)

The most useful kind of e-mail we receive comes from people asking for information on a specific topic; such requests help us to build our collection of sites. Teenagers who write to the IPL have been interested in emancipation, eating disorders, and depression, among other topics.

Some of the e-mail that results from patrons misunderstanding the nature and purpose of the divisions is funny. The Teen Division once received an e-mail message that consisted solely of algebra equations. Presumably the sender hoped that we would solve them all for him and send back the answers, ideally within the next five minutes.

Some messages illustrate the difficulty people have in understanding what Dave Carter in Chapter 2 calls "Web boundaries": where one site ends and another site begins. It's almost guaranteed that if you have a Web site that includes a large number of links to other sites, people will e-mail you to tell you that something on one of the sites you link to doesn't work, without realizing that you can't fix it because you don't maintain it.

A disturbing variant on the Web boundaries sort of e-mail is e-mail that takes you to task for content that is not on the sites that *you* link to, but is on the sites that the sites that you link to link to. (Confused yet? So were we.) As described in detail in Chapter 2, we once received a complaint about a site that was *five* levels of links away from the Teen Division. Many people now put disclaimers on their sites to the effect that their "for Kids Web site is not responsible for the content of links included on sites linked to from this page."

Some e-mail, of course, is advertisements. If you put a site together for children or young adults, expect to receive messages from kid-oriented commercial sites wanting you to link to them. You should also expect to receive messages that seem to be authentically from kids, but which just happen to recommend enthusiastically a particular product or site.

But the e-mail that is the hardest to answer—and yet perhaps the most important of all the mail we receive—is the mail from young adults with particular personal issues and concerns that they want to discuss. We have received mail from gay teens, teens suffering from eating disorders, teens who are pregnant, teens who are depressed and suicidal. In most cases, we try to refer the teens to sites that focus more directly on their problems. (See the Issues and Conflicts section of the Teen Division for some specific sites.) But in some cases, the teens continue writing after we have recommended other sites for them to visit—perhaps because we had actually responded to them. In these cases, I continue to respond, but only with very brief messages, frequently reiterating the site suggestions (and suggestions to talk to a counselor in person) that I had made previously. The teens eventually stop sending more e-mail.

E-mail like this, of course, raises a host of issues. Is it ethical to refer kids to Web sites that deal with personal problems? Would it be more appropriate simply to recommend that the patron speak to a counselor in person? Is receiving an e-mail message about a sensitive issue, such as sexuality, comparable to being approached about such an issue at the reference desk? Perhaps in many cases it is easier to type sensitive questions and mail them away into the ether than it is to approach a librarian about them in person. How to respond to messages about personal problems is yet another issue to think about when you are developing a site for kids or young adults.

Working with a Teen Advisory Board
The IPL Teen Division Advisory Board has the distinction of having been the first (and probably the only) teen advisory board to function entirely via electronic communication.

Figure 4-4. Teen Advisory Board Form.

Solicitation for Teen Advisory Board
http://www.ipl.org/teen/boardform.html

The Internet Public Library

Join Us!
The Internet Public Library Teen Division is looking for ten dedicated, creative people between the ages of 13 and 19 to serve on our Advisory Board. You do not have to be from the United States, but you need to be able to speak English.

What Do I Get Out Of It??
- Contribute to a popular website currently receiving around 100,000 hits a day
- Have a short biography of yourself appear in the Teen Division
- Interact with other Advisory Board members
- Learn about selecting and evaluating Internet resources
- Experience for your college application and/or resume

What Will I Do?
- Evaluate Web sites
- Contribute graphics and design ideas
- Help develop new projects for the Division.

We want the Division to be relevant to the information needs and wants of teenagers, and your input is the only way we can make that happen.

In return, the Division will be a space where you can experiment with new technology, make friends with other Board members from around the Internet, and get a broad audience for your work.

Before You Apply
You might want to read: IPL Teen Division Collection Development: Things You Need To Know and the IPL Teen Division Collection Development Plan. These documents have been written to help prospective Advisory Board members understand more about some of the work you'll be doing for the IPL Teen Division.

Figure 4-4. (Continued)

Remember

Your application is all the information we have about you. You may know that you're brilliant, and perfect for the Board, but we don't know that unless you convince us on your application. So do it!

To Apply

We need the following information about you:

NAME: _____

AGE: _____

ADDRESS, including street address, city, state or province, and country:

_____

_____

EMAIL ADDRESS: _____

URL of your homepage, if any (you don't need one to apply!):

_____

URL of your school's homepage, if any:

_____

How you access the Internet, in as much detail as possible. Include the kind of computer you use, the software you use to browse the Web, and any programs that you use to create graphics, multimedia or other Web content. Let us know if you connect from home, school, or both.

Do you have easy access to someone who can answer technical questions for you about using the Internet and/or creating content for the Internet?
          _____Yes _____No

Figure 4-4. (Continued)

Write a short essay (2000 words maximum) that includes:
- A critique of the Teen Division as it now exists. Take into consideration such aspects of the Division as: the graphic design, the subjects covered, the phrases used to describe each subject, and the entries contained in each subject area. Don't be afraid to be critical!
- A description of a Web project you would like to see in the Teen Division if you became an Advisory Board member.

If you don't want to send in your application via this form, feel free to send it to:

Internet Public Library
Teen Division Advisory Board Applications
Attn: Sara Ryan
550 East University
Ann Arbor, MI 48109–1092

Make sure to include all the information requested on the form if you send in your application by surface mail.

Important Note: You do not need to be an Internet expert to serve on the Advisory Board! But you do need to be comfortable working by yourself on the Internet, and experience creating HTML documents and/or other Web content is very helpful.

The deadline for applications for the Advisory Board has been extended to January 31, 1997. Advisory Board members will be notified by email.

I don't recommend functioning that way.

My hope, when I decided to solicit teens to join an advisory board, was that I would attract technologically sophisticated, talented, motivated teenagers. I did—and then I found out that they were already very busy with the sorts of other activities (theater, school literary magazines and newspapers, political organizations, sports, and religious groups) that you would expect a group of intelligent and creative teenagers to be engaged in. And because I had no face-to-face contact with them, I wasn't able to give them motivational carrots *or* sticks.

If you want to work with a teen advisory board on designing a teen-oriented Web site, use a combination of face-to-face meetings and electronic communication. Electronic communication is good for getting honest opinions—particularly if you can put up a form that will allow your board to comment anonymously about particularly difficult or controversial topics. Communicating electronically also definitely ups the "coolness factor" of being on a library teen advisory board. On the other hand, face-to-face communication helps to build relationships and the sense of being a team. (Plus, you can bring treats!)

The most obvious benefit of working with a teen advisory board on a Web site is, of course, having direct contact with the audience you want to reach. But working with an advisory board also means that they'll *advise* you—and you may not always agree with their advice.

Perhaps the most interesting aspect—as in the curse "May you live in interesting times"—of the IPL Teen Advisory Board's tenure was its influence on the kinds of sites included in the division. I found myself in a catch-22; I wanted input from teenagers, but frequently found myself disagreeing with their choices of good sites. For instance, several board members were interested in fashion—a topic that by its very nature implies commercialism—and one member chose to develop an entire "Style" section as her individual project. Similarly, another board member was interested in software, and reviewed a number of commercial sites whose main virtue was the fact that you could download some programs free of charge.

If you disagree violently with your board about individual Web sites, try to explain your disagreement in terms that they'll understand. Don't say, "This is a commercial site and its content is therefore unreliable"; say instead, "They're just trying to sell you something. Do you really think you can trust them to put up good information?" It's an excellent opportunity to do some instruction about how to evaluate Web sites. When I put the IPL Teen Advisory Board together, I wrote up introductory documents that explained what "collection development" was and how we would approach it for the IPL Teen Division. (See http://ipl.org:2000/teen/teencollqa.html and http://ipl.org:2000/teencolldevplan.html.) Think about writing similar documents for your own library, or even putting prospective board members through training in library jargon and library philosophy before they start working with you.

You may find that even after you do your best to educate your board, they're *still* convinced that you really need to link to the Nintendo site. You'll have to decide for yourself what to do in cases like this, but my own advice would be to go ahead and add the link. If you create an advisory board and then don't pay attention to what they tell you, your board members won't feel valued.

Publishing Original Content

Q. How do you make a small fortune in publishing?
A. Start with a large fortune.

The most ambitious youth services project tackled by the IPL was the production of *WebINK: Internet Newsletter for Kids*, a newsletter produced in both print and electronic form. Each issue of *WebINK* focused on a particular theme, and staff wrote articles about the theme and incorporated links to Web sites that kids could explore. The hope was that subscriptions to *WebINK* would help provide a stable funding base for the IPL.

The librarians, educators, and parents who subscribed to

WebINK found its combination of print and online content very useful. However, *WebINK* had almost no budget to publicize its existence to the people who would be best served by its offerings, and it was therefore extraordinarily difficult to attract subscribers.

If you want to publish some form of magazine or newsletter as a component of your services for youth, here are a few options you could consider:

- Treat it as a public relations expense. Use it as a way to publicize *all* your programs, not just your Web services.
- Target a very specific audience—say, Spanish-speaking kids who are learning English—and seek a grant to fund the publication of the newsletter for a designated amount of time.
- Don't do a print form of the publication at all. This will save you a lot of money and will decrease the types of expertise required to produce the publication.
- Partner with an organization that is already producing a publication targeted at kids and do special features or columns about the Web services for youth that your library offers.

Plus Ça Change . . .

The most important aspect of the IPL's services to youth has remained unchanged throughout all the various manifestations of the Youth and Teen Divisions and every issue of *WebINK*, and that is, quite simply, the commitment to *serve* young people. To continue the highest quality service, the IPL Youth and Teen Divisions rely on the dozens of e-mail messages from young people for site selection, philosophy, and ideas for future services.

WHAT TO DO IN YOUR LIBRARY

For public librarians these days, it sometimes seems that all the complex issues and challenges that surround youth services in the Internet environment reduce to the question of whether you're going to install filtering software on the public access terminals in your library's children's room. If you're trying to make this choice, I recommend that you investigate TIFAP, The Internet Filtering Assessment Project (www.bluehighways. com/filters), and *A Practical Guide to Internet Filters* by Karen Schneider (New York, Neal-Schuman, 1997), which builds on TIFAP's work.

It is also imperative that your library not make its decision in a vacuum. Many of the people who are the most concerned about young people and their use of the Internet are the least informed about the nature of the technology. They've seen a few alarmist television features and read some equally chilling articles in the popular press, and have formed all their opinions in light of information that is both biased and inadequate. Recognize that you will need to educate your community, and that means that you have to be educated first. Start the filtering debate and discussion before it is brought to you by people whose minds are already made up. Involve community leaders, educators, parents, *and young people*. It could be very informative, for instance, to have members of the local chapter of the National Honor Society prepare a presentation about the ways they have used the Internet in the past year.

The IPL has not had to consider the filtering question in quite the same way as other public libraries, because the IPL is both blessed and cursed with the lack of an easily defined community of users. We are not bound by the community standards of any particular community—or vocal subset thereof. This characteristic has allowed us the opportunity to stand wholeheartedly on the side of open access to information and intellectual freedom. The Teen Division is particularly well supplied with links to informative sites in the controversial areas of health and sexuality information, and has not removed these links, although they have been challenged on more than one occasion. However, we have been especially concerned about the dangers of site-blocking software. The IPL could be blocked by some of the programs currently available, because some of our annotations contain keywords that the programs flag as offensive. Users who could benefit greatly from the library's offerings might never even learn of its existence. Fortunately, these programs are not in wide use.

But neither does the IPL have the advantages that come from working with a particular, geographically defined community. Other public librarians, armed with specific knowledge about the demographics of their communities, can create much more precisely targeted services for youth. Included below are some ideas for such projects.

Local history. Many schools have curriculum units based around local history. Sometimes kids are required to interview senior citizens of the community to find out what their town was like 40 or 50 years ago, or to study and photograph old buildings or natural features. Kids could easily type up the interviews (or record them if the appropriate equipment is available), and scan the photographs, and build up a substantial resource that would simultaneously offer the kids a chance to see their work on the Web and provide the larger community with useful information. Such information is particularly appropriate in the context of the increasingly popular vision of public libraries as community information centers.

Young adults as technology teachers. Make use of the technological expertise of young adults. Train them how to be effective instructors, and use them as assistants in large classes offered for the public, or have them lead classes for their peers or for younger children.

Partnerships with schools. Schools desperately need help providing kids not only with instruction in how to use Internet-based information resources, but also with projects that will allow them to use the resources in a meaningful way. If the kids are going to learn that using the Internet for research doesn't mean cutting and pasting information from the Web into their research papers, they need to develop an understanding of intellectual property, and they also need to learn how to recognize wrong information even when it's presented slickly.

Librarians can help not only by building collections of good sites for the kids to use, but by collecting examples of sites that provide wrong information, and developing exercises where kids have to check multiple sources and figure out which site has the right answer. Librarians can also collect examples of different sites that use some of the same (non–clip art) graphics, and challenge the kids to track down which site actually originated the graphics. There is actually no limit to the ways public librarians can work in partnership with schools. And there is room for all levels of partnership, from very basic agreements (such as one stating that the library will offer space on its Web site for school-sponsored art and writing contests each year) to a full-scale collaboration on major curriculum units in which the librarians create customized "Webliographies" and present training sessions for the students on how to use search engines and evaluate Web sites.

Community calendar. Use space on the library Web site not only to publicize library programs for young people, but also for programs offered by other organizations focused on young people.

Story hour. If you're hiring a renowned storyteller to come into your library, negotiate in the contract that the storyteller will record one story in digital form for the library Web site. The storyteller will probably be glad for the additional publicity, and you will have added a valuable resource to your digital collection. Do the same thing if a children's author makes an appearance, or a musician. Also consider having kids record stories and poetry that they've written.

Some of these ideas may sound daunting because they require more advanced technology, or greater facility with technology, than your library currently has. Consider partnerships with locally based businesses. For example, a firm that sells computer hardware may be willing to donate equipment to the library, particularly if the owner of the firm has a child who could record a story for the library Web site.

Also recognize that these are only a few possible ideas. Probably the most useful strategy is to think about the programs you already have in your library for young people, and consider how you might be able to incorporate Internet-based elements into them.

OTHER POPULATIONS

Although the focus of this chapter has been on services to young people, it is possible to extrapolate from the concepts and examples presented to conceptualize services to other populations. For instance, if your library wants to develop Internet-based services especially for senior citizens, you could follow similar strategies: figure out the design needs specific to the target audience and build pages accordingly, gather input from senior citizens about topics of interest, and potentially involve senior citizens in the construction and maintenance of the resources designed for them. You could also extend the ideas to the creation of services for the disabled, or for specific ethnic and cultural minorities.

The most important idea to take away from this chapter is that using the Internet in the ways discussed above is a new way of thinking about services, and the services can be implemented in new and exciting ways, but they're still services. And you are extremely well qualified to figure out the best way to serve young people in your community.

NOTES

1. Readers interested in a description of the creation of the IPL Youth Division by the original coordinator of the division should read Josie Barnes Parker's article, "Internet Public Library Youth Division," *Journal of Youth Services in Libraries*, 9(3): 270–279, Spring 1996.
2. Many Web sites designed for kids use these strategies now, but it's important to remember when this design was being developed. This was design for a Web where many users still viewed pages with the original NCSA Mosaic browser—Netscape had only recently achieved a dominant market share—and where the fastest modem speed most users could hope for was 14.4kb per second.
3. See, for example, Lynda Weinman, *Coloring Web Graphics: Master Color and Image File Formats for the Web* (Indianapolis, Ind.: New Riders Publishing, 1996).
4. In fact, there are at least a few teenagers who read and post to YALSA-BK, the book discussion list maintained by the Young Adult Library Services Association.
5. Readers interested in a more extended discussion of the creation of the IPL Teen Division should read the paper that Samantha Bailey and I presented at the 1996 Annual Meeting of the Internet Society, "Making Web Space for Young Adults: Issues and Process—A Case Study of the Internet Public Library Teen Division," available online at www.isoc.org/
   .

Chapter 5

Establishing Online Reference Services

Nettie Lagace

I've never thought of reference desks, or reference sections of libraries, as static, quiet, stable places. Libraries are for users; I think that reference desks are where the "real work" of the library gets done—where patrons and librarians interact, where librarians, experts on the sources and inner workings of the library, help patrons find the precise answers to their questions, or identify particular sources for further exploration of a topic of interest (or need).

The library's reference center is also where librarians can observe firsthand what users need from the library, how they interact with library material, and whether they find what they are seeking (and when they don't, what went wrong or prevented a successful answer). In the reference center librarians can observe where users are running into difficulty with tools and interfaces and what tools and sources are most useful and popular. This is where librarians can take note of how patrons approach information mazes, and pass on that information to catalogers and system designers to help build better pathways and organization schemes.

We built the IPL Reference Center and established an e-mail reference system because we didn't want the IPL to be a Web site floating all by itself in cyberspace; we felt we needed to have contact with our patrons on a regular basis. We wanted to create a mechanism so that we could hear from people, to know what they wanted to gain from the Internet and how they anticipated this amazing new source would affect their lives, how they viewed libraries and librarians in general, and how they could more effectively use and support their own libraries.

We also wanted to use our skills to help people, like all librarians do. "Reference" can mean a collection of resources that answer questions, but it also means experienced professionals who can help with personalized guidance to those resources, and we wanted the people who visit the IPL to know that there are people who work to provide those resources in the collections, and who also have an interest in knowing that our users are finding what they need.

Nine students comprised the original IPL Reference group in January 1995. We decided at our first meeting that interactive services were essential to supporting the mission of the IPL, and that we could not call ourselves a true public library without them. As we ventured into the as-yet-mostly-uncharted territory of electronic operations, we decided to use as our model the well-understood process of running a traditional reference desk: providing a visible contact point where patrons can obtain help in navigating the library's spaces, evaluating resources, and finding answers to their questions. We concluded that reference services are as useful in a virtual environment as in a physical one, and that to fulfill our mission we would provide them to our patrons as far as we were able.

SORTING THROUGH SEAS OF INFORMATION

We were all Internet-savvy library students; we had fun using the Internet and found it to be an extremely rich resource to answer research and reference queries. But we also were properly wary of it and we knew how it is not easily navigable; paths disappear as often as new ones crop up. The Internet is both marvelous (it welcomes everyone's contributions and creations, no matter how big or small) and terrible (there's often no order to these contributions and they may not have the quality or authoritativeness of traditional print sources). There are almost always several approaches to take when tackling a question and using the Internet to answer it.

HOW THE IPL REFERENCE CENTER HANDLES QUESTIONS

The IPL Reference Center would not exist without the collaborative efforts of the many volunteer librarians and library students who are willing to contribute their time to answer questions for people whom they never see or meet in person. Our internally developed software system, QRC, is also integral to the operation; QRC allows librarians to work together to answer questions, even though they may not be working in the same place or at the same time.

As explained in more detail below, the basic process is that patrons submit questions via our Web form or through e-mail, and these questions are automatically routed to the IPL's own specially developed software system called QRC. IPL staff and librarian volunteers can then log into QRC through their own Web browsers and choose questions to answer from the list of those that have come in. We send answers back to the patrons via e-mail. (See Figure 5-1.)

Volunteer librarians may log into QRC on the Web at any time that's convenient to them—while they are tending their own reference desks at quiet times, during lunch hour, checking in after work, or even perhaps from home late at night. They view a list of questions currently waiting to be answered, labeled with keywords and subject headings assigned by the reference administrator, and "claim" the questions they want to work on and reply to. Many of our volunteers have commented that in contrast to their jobs at "regular" reference desks where they must answer every question asked of them, one of the best features of working at the IPL is the opportunity to choose for themselves which questions to work on; they can answer ques-

Figure 5-1. Ask a Question Introductory Page.

the Internet Public Library

Reference Question Form

Reminder:

We are not able to perform lengthy research. However we can provide brief answers to factual questions or suggestions for locations and sources which might help to answer your question.

PLEASE READ! About the IPL Ask-A-Question Service

Before you ask a reference question, please check to see if your question is in the Frequently Asked Reference Questions list. You could save yourself, and us, a lot of time.

IPL Reference Question

Contact Information: Tell us about yourself.

Please make sure that your e-mail address is correctly entered, so that we can respond to your question. (Example: fluggly@aol.com) If you do not enter a valid Internet e-mail address, we will not be able to respond to your question.

Type in your name:
Your e-mail address:
Your location (City, State/Country):
This information won't be useful after (date):

The Subject Area of the Question: (click to see list -- choose one)

(None Selected)

Question: Write your question in the following space. **If you have more than one question, please use a new form for each question.** Please include the following.

1. Describe the question or problem to be searched. Be as complete and specific as possible. A human being will read your question -- please use complete sentences! The more you tell us, the better our answer will be.
2. If possible, describe how you will use this information.

Will you use this information for a school assignment?

○ Yes
○ No

Figure 5-1. (Continued)

Keywords: Provide any keywords, significant terms, phrases, synonyms, acronyms, etc. that describe your subject specifically in the following space.

Type of answer preferred: (choose one of the following)

- ○ A brief factual answer to your question
- ○ Some ideas for sources to consult for exploration

Type of Internet resources that you can use: (check acceptable formats)

- ☐ World Wide Web - with graphics/multimedia
- ☐ World Wide Web - text only
- ☐ Gopher
- ☐ FTP
- ☐ E-mail/Listserv
- ☐ Any format

Sources Consulted: List any resources on the net or off that you've already consulted (so we don't duplicate your attempts). Don't forget to try using our Ready Reference Collection and your local library to answer your question.

Reminder: Please take a moment to re-check the e-mail address you are submitting to us, since it is **impossible** for us to communicate with you unless it is correct. Thanks!

[Submit Question]   [Reset ToDefault Values]

If you have problems using this form, you can also submit a question by e-mail. For instructions, consult the E-Mail Guidelines.

Return to Ask a Question | IPL Reference Center | IPL Lobby

the Internet Public Library - = - http://www.ipl.org/ - = - ipl@ipl.org
Last updated Nov 01, 1996.

tions that they have a personal interest in, or ones that are within their own subject specialty.

OUR SYSTEM IS CALLED QRC

It's impossible to explain how IPL reference works without first providing an overview of QRC—the acronym doesn't stand for anything, and is pronounced "quirk." QRC manages the entire process of receiving mail, sorting and labeling it, claiming and answering it, and finally archiving it. QRC was written by Michael McClennen, the IPL system administrator. In 1995 Michael observed the original reference group struggling to adapt a bulletin board program, HyperNews (whose code was freely available), to an interactive reference process that really required more dynamism and flexibility.

We needed a program that could be used by librarians in diverse geographical locations, as well as by library students at the University of Michigan working in different campus computing labs or from home. We needed a program that would prevent duplicate work, but one that would allow all the far-flung librarians to see at a glance the status of questions. Administrators needed to know which questions had been answered, and which ones were unclaimed and in danger of falling through the cracks.

We wanted patrons to be able to interact with our system via both Web forms and e-mail, and we wanted our volunteer librarians to be able to access those submissions from anywhere in the world without needing special software. We couldn't use Lotus Notes or another commercial product because we rely on the generosity of our volunteers' time; we couldn't ask them to purchase another piece of software, let alone worry about what kind of hardware or software they already had, besides a good Web browser and a connection to the Internet.

The final item on our wish list was a system that would archive answered questions. In the early days of the IPL, we anticipated that we would receive many duplicate questions; we wanted to be able to reuse our work easily. We also wanted to be able to extract quantitative and qualitative data so that we could refine and improve different aspects of the reference process, as we grew more accustomed to the nature of "virtual reference."

Michael made sure that QRC met all of our requirements. Within a few months he had written QRC, tested and fixed its major bugs, and installed it on our server, and we have been rolling with it ever since, with some modifications, additions, and improvements invented by Michael along the way.

The idea behind QRC is that it is a program to facilitate communication and collaboration between all the people involved in a reference transaction. It not only provides a communication channel between IPL patrons and librarians, but it also allows librarians to coordinate their activity and to share their work. As discussed in greater depth later in this chapter, in order to answer a question adequately, a librarian has to be able to engage in a dialogue with the patron—to request more information if necessary, to receive the patron's follow-up messages, and to send an answer back. Efficient handling of questions also requires coordination among the librarians. One librarian may post a partial answer, either directly to the patron or back to the QRC bulletin board, and ask for help from someone with more experience in the subject area. QRC also has mechanisms that prevent two librarians from trying to answer the same question at the same time, which wastes work and may confuse a patron.

At the IPL, we have a few levels of question-handling; we have developed a triage process, where one librarian or library student with access permissions uses QRC to sort the daily mail received in the main reference inbox. This person separates the real questions from mistakes and spam e-mail, and further sorts the questions into two categories, one containing straightforward factual questions, and one containing questions that are better answered with source suggestions.

QRC generally resembles a Web "bulletin board" program. We've set up several different categories within QRC to hold our e-mail correspondence and queries. Each original message is kept as an "item," to which are added all of the subsidiary messages that are generated in its lifetime as an active question: responses from librarians and from the patron, comments posted for the benefit of other librarians, and automatically generated tracking messages that preserve the history of the item. When the administrator "governing" an item finally closes it out—after it's been fully answered and any final correspondence (thank-yous and other notes) has been appended—he or she can mark it for inclusion in an archive, from which it can be recalled in response to queries. All access to QRC is password protected—that is, aside from messages from patrons posted through our Web forms and sent to our e-mail addresses, naturally.

Once volunteer librarians have logged onto QRC via the Web, they choose a category in which to view items, for example Factual Questions or Source Questions. They may then check on the status of items that they are working on (to see if the patron has sent in a follow-up message) or view items that have been newly processed by the IPL reference administrator. They may use QRC functions to "claim" an item (which prevents others from working on it), respond to the person who sent in the item (the response is automatically sent to the patron by e-mail), post a comment, and so on. An administrator has additional provileges to transfer items between categories, mark them for archiving, and change their attributes.

QRC has proven to be a very flexible system, easily configured to handle different kinds of communications tasks. At the IPL, we use QRC for much more than our reference operation; we also use it for all our general correspondence, and for recording progress and notes for any particular group projects that we may work on, such as the Native American Authors database or the new Online Literary Criticism collection. We have also begun testing QRC in other library environments to see how well it adapts to different users and functions. So far, it has been successfully tested in academic, public, and special libraries, and we are continuing to develop QRC into a product that librarians everywhere can install and use to extend their existing services into the digital realm, and to develop new services that take advantage of the power of the unique medium of the global network.

THOUSANDS OF ANSWERED QUESTIONS

We intended from the very beginning of the IPL project to create a searchable database of answered questions. Over two years later, this database is finally very near realization. There were many obstacles associated with making such a database available for use by a diverse array of librarians or by the general Internet public. For example, questions often come in with personal information scattered throughout the text, keeping us from making the messages available until we could figure out a way to mask or remove this information.

And surprisingly, in the several thousand questions that we've received from IPL patrons over the past two years, there are very few repeat questions, certainly far fewer than we anticipated we would encounter in the early days when we planned our database of answered questions. However, although they may not ask exactly the same questions, IPL patrons often ask similar kinds of questions, and we have authored a few dozen FARQs (frequently answered reference questions) and an ever-increasing number of reference pathfinders, or guides, to try to answer questions more efficiently and quickly. These FARQs and pathfinders are also available to the public at the IPL Reference Center, and they are continually updated and checked for accuracy and completeness as new Web resources make themselves available and others disappear forever, as is the way of the Web.

THE QUESTIONS WE CAN'T ANSWER

Running a worldwide reference service is incredibly exciting and fun. However, one of the most regrettable aspects of the IPL services is that we don't have enough staff and volunteers to answer all of the questions that arrive in our mailbox. The number of questions we receive varies depending on whether school is in session and on any recent IPL publicity, but it usually ranges from 25 to 35 questions per day. We try to accept at least 20 per day which will be answered by volunteer staff, but again, this number varies depending on how many questions are still unanswered from previous days. Each day, an IPL reference administrator makes a first pass through the questions that have arrived in the past 24 hours, accepting as many as possible and posting them for librarians to read and answer, discarding spam and mistakenly directed messages, and rejecting questions that we cannot accept because we've reached our "quota" for the day. Each message sent to the IPL receives a polite, pre-composed response that lets the patron know that we are either working on his or her question or that we cannot answer it and it should be resubmitted later or taken to a local library for further help.

One way to help solve the problem of receiving too many questions would be to reduce the scope of the service. Other question-answering services have had more success in limiting their services; they lay out restrictions or intended audiences at the very beginning of the process, before users ever submit a form. I was never able to define successfully one "type" of IPL user whose questions we would or should concentrate on answering. Would we answer only questions from children? Only questions from other librarians? Only questions submitted by people new to the Internet? We continually want to attract volunteer librarians to participate in the operation and further cultivation of our service, and one of our "selling" points to librarians is that we receive questions of all kinds, from people of all kinds. I felt that, in order to attract the labor we needed to answer the questions, it was important for us to continue to invite the variety of questions themselves.

And besides, public libraries are for everyone in their communities, not just for one specific type of person. We encourage and advertise a breadth of collections and projects to include in the library; thus it would be unfair to discourage or limit the breadth of questions that IPL users submit. Part of the excitement of the IPL is its mission to include all Internet users, and indeed, we want to attract as wide a variety of patrons to our library as possible.

So, we manage. Every day the IPL reference administrator "eyeballs" the current "answer rate" and adjusts the number of questions accepted, depending on how quickly librarians and library students are dispensing with the "current" batch of questions; if questions are moving slowly—taking awhile to be claimed and answered—the number accepted will be smaller than on a day when questions are flying through the process. And we send out general news announcements to our e-mail list of volunteers, to remind them that the IPL is operating with their gracious help (and that it's great when they check back in).

PROFESSIONAL LIBRARIANS AND STUDENTS

When we planned the IPL Reference Center and originally anticipated "500 questions a day," we wanted to do much of the work ourselves, because the project was our idea and our responsibility, but we also wanted to solicit the input and help of professional librarians from other institutions and subject backgrounds—partly because we needed the labor, but also because we intended to create as well-rounded an expert reference staff as possible. We knew already from experience with Internet listservs and newsgroups that sharing information between colleagues was one of the functions that the Internet fulfilled best, and that if we could successfully publicize the IPL to other librarians, the IPL could be a place for them to share tips, sources, and learning experiences, all the while answering questions for Internet users.

We posted a call for volunteer librarians on about half a dozen library-related listservs, asking for help from librarians, library students, and paraprofessionals who work at reference desks.

SOME CHARACTERISTICS OF E-MAIL REFERENCE SERVICES

The IPL provides a place for anyone to ask a question—about anything. We try to answer these questions as completely as possible, and if we can't, we provide further leads and sources for the patron to consult. The procedure is not terribly complicated—it's a simple two-way, back-and-forth, e-mail transaction. But often there are "facets" contained in individual questions that are not so straightforward, and it's possible to interpret these parts of the communication in a number of different ways. For example, if a person sends an extremely brief message, does it mean she doesn't know anything about her topic? Does it mean she hates to type? Does it mean she's doing something else at that particular time and just wants to send her message as quickly as possible? If you've never met or seen the person who is asking you a question, non-real-time communication makes some things about answering questions easier, and some things worse. You have to identify the barriers to effective question answering in this particular communications medium, and construct mechanisms to compensate for what is missing. There are benefits in e-mail too, of course, and making the most of them can help to balance out the problems.

E-mail is a time-delayed text interaction between two people who have possibly (probably, in the case of the IPL) never met. As in the "real world," patrons are usually unaware of the "auxiliary information" that a librarian needs in order to answer a question efficiently: How soon do you need an answer? What will you use this information for? What format would you find acceptable? In a face-to-face reference interview, a librarian can ask these questions immediately or discern them in other more subtle ways, but the time delay caused by e-mail communication prevents the give-and-take of a conventional reference interview.

IPL staff have observed that, probably because of the time delays of e-mail exchanges (as well as the fact that the IPL is a

Figure 5-2. Current Ask a Question Form.

◆ the Internet Public Library

IPL Ask A Question Form

IPL Reference Question

Reminder:

We are not able to perform lengthy research. However we can provide brief answers to factual questions or suggestions for locations and sources which might help to answer your question.

PLEASE READ! About the IPL Ask-A-Question Service

Before you ask a reference question, please check to see if your question is in the Frequently Asked Reference Questions list. You could save yourself, and us, a lot of time.

---

1 **What is your name?**

What is your email address?

If you don't give us your correct, complete Internet email address (example: fluggly@aol.com), we can't send you an answer to your question.

Where do you live? (City/State/Country)

We can usually help you better if we know where you live, and how far away you are from the resources we may recommend to you.

---

2 **I won't need this information after:** _____ (date)

Click here if you are in a hurry.

---

3 **The Subject Area of the Question:** (click to see list -- choose one)

(None Selected) ▼

---

4 **Please tell us your question.**
A human being will read your question -- please use complete sentences!
The more you tell us, the better our answer will be. What do you already know about your subject or question?

---

5 **How will you use this information?** Why are you asking your question?
If you're just curious, that's ok, but it really helps librarians to know this part! Sometimes we can use our subject knowledge and imaginations to think of other places to look for answers and information, if we know how you will use it or what you want to get out of the answer.

Figure 5-2.   (Continued)

Will you use this information for a school assignment? ○ Yes ○ No

Are you: ☐ A librarian? ☐ A teacher? ☐ A businessperson?

---

6 Type of answer preferred: (choose one of the following)

○ A brief factual answer to your question

○ Some ideas for sources to consult for exploration:

☐ Internet sources ☐ Print sources ☐ I don't care which kind

Sometimes the information you want isn't available on the Internet, but might be available through a library near you. We can almost always get you started, at least.

---

7 Sources Consulted:

Please list any places on the Net or off that you've already checked regarding your question. We don't want to duplicate your attempts. Don't forget to try using our Ready Reference Collection and your local library to answer your question.

---

8 SEND IT!

Reminder: Please take a moment to re-check the e-mail address you are submitting to us, since it is **impossible** for us to communicate with you unless it is correct. Thanks!

Please confirm your email address.

    Submit Question to IPL Librarians   Reset Form To Default Values

If you have problems using this form, you can also submit a question by e-mail. For instructions, consult the E-Mail Guidelines.

Return to Ask a Question | IPL Reference Center | IPL Lobby

---

the Internet Public Library - = - http://www.ipl.org/ - = - ipl@ipl.org
Last updated Jun 5, 1998.

volunteer activity for many rather than a concrete part of their day-to-day work), IPL librarians send relatively few clarifying e-mail messages back to patrons, although administrators encourage librarians to clarify questions whenever possible before starting work. IPL librarians have been reluctant to consume even more time and possibly frustrate the patron by sending him or her these auxiliary, follow-up questions rather than *any* answer to the original question. In our experience, librarians—IPL administrators included—will typically pull together a package of material that might be what the patron needs, bundle it into an e-mail message, and send it off. As a result, the patron will usually have to assume a greater role in pointing out where the answer is deficient, or where clarification is needed.

THE QUESTION ITSELF

Is it always clear what the patron is asking? Of course not. In many cases, the patron may not know how best to express his or her information need. It has been written that in a reference exchange, the librarian is trying to force the person asking a question to describe something he or she knows little or nothing about—what a difficult task! How could it possibly be easy via e-mail?

E-mail reference can remove the niceties and strip a reference transaction right down to its bare bones: just the question. Or at least what the patron thinks his or her question is, and one of the most basic tenets of reference work is that patrons almost never start out with their "real question." Since the benefit of "real time" is missing in e-mail reference, the librarian cannot reply, "Uh-huh, go on, tell me more, keep talking," and simultaneously throw keywords into the OPAC—or a Web search engine. As much as possible needs to be laid out up front, while the patron is filling out the reference form.

We designed our question intake form (www.ipl.org/ref/QUE/ RefFormQRC.html or see Figure 5-2) to try to elicit as much information as possible from the patron *before* the librarian starts work. As a result, our form is much more elaborate than simply a text box where the patron can type his or her question. In the summer of 1997 we substantially modified this form from its previous incarnation, which had been in use since we opened in March 1995. (Figure 5-3 depicts the original form.) We used HTML tables to make its layout more attractive, and added colorful number buttons to make it easier to follow.

But we also made it a longer form. Our original form included a field for Keywords, where we hoped patrons would generate their own online searching vocabulary. This field never worked quite the way it was intended, as patrons tended, quite natu-

Figure 5-3. Original Ask a Question Form

Archive: **Answered Reference Questions**, article 5984:
SCI: Gestation/fertility of goose eggs

Author: ███████████████
Posted: Sat, 06 Apr 1996 14:28:43
Category: 726ref.cat
Status: ANSWERED,RECV_MSG

You are now signed on as **Nettie Lagace (lagace)**

Return to Archive File | Category Archive | Top Level Archive | view the User Manual

```
Question:

I would like to know the gestation period of a Canadian
goose egg. My daughter recently found one abandoned and is
trying to hatch it. I would also like to know how to tell
if it is fertile. Any other information regarding this
subject will be greatly appreciated.

Level: basic
Keywords:
Sources:
Area: Other/Misc

Keywords: egg, gestation, waterfowl
Sources+Consulted: Grolier's Multimedia Encylopedia
answer: factual
Not+needed+after:
location: RI
email+list: yes
from:  ███████████
```

Responses:

1: Set STATUS to ACCEPTED Sun, 07 Apr 1996 12:13:02
        by Nettie Lagace (lagace@umich.edu)

2: CHANGE SUBJECT to "SCI: Gestation/fertility of goose eggs" from "IPL Reference Question" Sun, 07 Apr 1996 12:13:02
        by Nettie Lagace (lagace@umich.edu)

3: SENT standard message "accept" to Author Sun, 07 Apr 1996 12:13:02
        by Nettie Lagace (lagace@umich.edu)

4: TRANSFER to "General Reference Questions TBA" from "Incoming Articles from Mail and HTTP" Sun, 07 Apr 1996 12:13:03
        by Nettie Lagace (lagace@umich.edu)

5: CLAIMED Sun, 07 Apr 1996 20:07:30
        by Cameron Trowbridge (cambridg@umich.edu)

6: Re: SCI: Gestation/fertility of goose eggs (sent to original author) Sun, 07 Apr 1996 20:23:17
        by Cameron Trowbridge (cambridg@umich.edu)

```
        Hello Debbie!

        The gestation period of a Canadian Goose egg is 150 days.  I found the
        information in a wonderful source called _The birder's handbook : a field
        guide to the natural history of North American birds : including all species that
         regularly breed north of Mexico_ by Paul Ehrlich (New York : Simon & Schuster,
        c1988.

        Hope this helps! Thanks for using the IPL!

        > Question: ... [17 lines quoted]
```

7: Set STATUS to ANSWERED Sun, 07 Apr 1996 20:23:17
        by Cameron Trowbridge (cambridg@umich.edu)

8: Re: SCI: Gestation/fertility of goose eggs (sent to original author) Sun, 07 Apr 1996 20:47:13
        by Cameron Trowbridge (cambridg@umich.edu)

Figure 5-3.   (Continued)

Debbie,

I realized I didn't answer the second part of your question! You can tell if
the egg is fertile by holding it up to a bright light source and looking for
the silhouette of the embryo.   You might also be interested to know the diet
of the Canadian Goose which consists mainly of shoots, roots, and seeds of
grass and sedges, bulbs, grain, berries insects, crustaceans and mollusks.

I also found the following Web sites which offer information about the Canadian
Goose:

http://www.ns.net/~pallen/nature/bird.html
http://informns.k12.mn.us/~moen/october/Canadagoose.html

Including this one in which the author talks about raising a Canadian Goose:

http://path.upmc.edu/~field/birds.html

Hope this will be helpful!   Good luck!

> Question: ... [17 lines quoted]

9: Set STATUS to ANSWERED Sun, 07 Apr 1996 20:47:13
      by Cameron Trowbridge (cambridg@umich.edu)

10: TRANSFER to "Questions answered by ILS 726 class members" from "General Reference Questions TBA" Mon, 08 Apr 1996 02:43:18
      by Nettie Lagace (lagace@umich.edu)

11: Re: SCI: Gestation/fertility of goose eggs [ref#5984] Mon, 08 Apr 1996 20:34:30
      by u̶̶̶̶̶̶̶̶̶̶̶̶̶̶̶)

From: ▆▆▆▆▆▆▆
Date: Mon, 8 Apr 1996 16:29:48 -0400
To: iplref@umich.edu
cc: ▆▆▆▆▆▆
Subject: Re: SCI: Gestation/fertility of goose eggs [ref#5984]

Thank you so much for the information about out little goose. We held the egg
up to a bright light like you suggested and as far as we can tell it is
fertile. I am also looking into your sources to make sure that we do this
right. If it hatches, I'll let you know.
Again, thank you....you were a tremendous help.

Debbie

Return to Archive File | Category Archive | Top Level Archive | view the User Manual rally, to expect the librarian to be able to generate additional searching terms or synonyms. Usually, the keyword field, as submitted by patrons, contained either no words at all, or words that already existed in the body of the question, rather than any subject-specific vocabulary or helpful lingo.

So we removed this underused field entirely, and added a required Reason field: "Why do you want to know? How will you use this information? What do you already know about your question?" We configured our form's submission script to check this field to make sure that it contains at least some text, and the form cannot be successfully submitted until the patron provides information there. We felt that if librarians at least knew the purpose behind the question, we'd be that much closer to a better answer, or better suggestions for sources or research strategies, even if the patron was not able to describe the question precisely.

This attempt to find the question behind the question works in e-mail as well as it often does in "real life"; even though some responses in the reason field still remain vaguely phrased ("for school" or "my mom wants to know" are typical), on the whole, its addition has benefited question intake immeasurably. The improvement was dramatic and immediate; we noticed right away how much "better" our questions were, and we felt much more confident steering people in our e-mail answers. I believe, as in a face-to-face reference exchange, that prodding patrons to describe the "outside edges" of their information need can help in defining what remains to be discovered. (Perhaps the process is a little like artists cutting away the parts of a sculpture that don't belong.)

When we lengthened our form we also annotated several of the fields, to try to explain our reference interview process. We wanted patrons to know how we were going to use the information. For example, we added a note to the field where we ask the patron where he or she lives, to explain that it helps to be able to direct users to resources close to them. We were concerned that the form' length might present a barrier for or serve

Figure 5-4. Sample IPL Reference Question and Answer I

Archive: Answered Reference Questions, article 18370:
GEN: Time difference between Moscow and Detroit

Author: ~~█████████~~
Posted: Sun, 02 Mar 1997 19:03:26
Category: 726ref.cat
Status: ANSWERED,SENT_MSG

You are now signed on as Nettie Lagace (lagace)

Return to Archive File | Category Archive | Top Level Archive | view the User Manual

---

```
Question:

Please tell me the time difference between Moscow,Russia
compared to Detroit,Mich. in hours.
For future reference, where would I find this info again.
Regards,
Pat

Area: Humanities
Sources+Consulted: columbia encylopedia, reference pages, web, etc.
School: No
Any: yes
Answer: factual
Not+needed+after: 4/30/97
Location: dbn,mich
```

Responses:

1: Set STATUS to ACCEPTED Tue, 04 Mar 1997 11:39:42
    by Nettie Lagace (lagace@umich.edu)

2: CHANGE SUBJECT to "GEN: Time difference between Moscow and Detroit" from "IPL Reference Question" Tue, 04 Mar 1997 11:39:42
    by Nettie Lagace (lagace@umich.edu)

3: SENT standard message "accept" to Author Tue, 04 Mar 1997 11:39:42
    by Nettie Lagace (lagace@umich.edu)

4: TRANSFER to "General Reference Questions TBA" from "Incoming Articles from Mail and HTTP" Tue, 04 Mar 1997 11:39:43
    by Nettie Lagace (lagace@umich.edu)

5: CLAIMED Tue, 04 Mar 1997 13:51:46
    by Bryan Blank (bblank@si.umich.edu)

6: Re: GEN: Time difference between Moscow and Detroit (sent to original author) Tue, 04 Mar 1997 13:53:00
    by Bryan Blank (bblank@si.umich.edu)

```
    Pat,
            Here is a URL that will tell you the timer differences if you ever
    need to check again:
     http://www.stud.unit.no/USERBIN/steffent/verdensur.pl

    and so you know...Moscow is 8 hours ahead of us.

    I just compared Moscow time to New York to get it.

    be good
    -bryan

    > Question: ... [13 lines quoted]
```

7: Set STATUS to ANSWERED Tue, 04 Mar 1997 13:53:00
    by Bryan Blank (bblank@si.umich.edu)

8: TRANSFER to "Questions answered by ILS 726 class members" from "General Reference Questions TBA" Wed, 05 Mar 1997 10:26:57
    by Nettie Lagace (lagace@umich.edu)

Return to Archive File | Category Archive | Top Level Archive | view the User Manual

Figure 5-5. Sample IPL Reference Question and Answer II

Archive: Answered Reference Questions, article 26304:
SCI: Days of the week for past dates

Author: ~~████████████~~)
Posted: Sun, 03 Aug 1997 22:26:41
Category: refgen.cat
Status: ANSWERED,SENT_MSG

You are now signed on as **Nettie Lagace (lagace)**

Return to <u>Archive File</u> | <u>Category Archive</u> | <u>Top Level Archive</u> | view the <u>User Manual</u>

```
Location: Hilton, NY  USA
Area: Other/Misc

Question: Dear Library Staff:
On what days of the week did the following dates fall:
October 1, 1960
July 30, 1969
and September 1, 1993?
Thank you for researching this information for me.
Sincerely,
```
~~███~~
```
Reason:

I am expecting my second baby am interested in finding out
what days of the week my family was born.

Sources-Consulted: I haven't consulted any sources yet and am not quite sure
where to start.

Answer-type: factual
Format3: doesn't matter
School: No
Teacher: yes
```

Responses:

1: CHANGE AUTHADDR to "~~████████~~" from "~~████████~~" Thu, 07 Aug 1997 09:57:45
    by Nettie Lagace (lagace@umich.edu)

2: Re: IPL Reference Question (sent to original author) Sat, 09 Aug 1997 17:19:56
    by Lorri Mon (lmon@si.umich.edu)

```
Hi ███,

Thanks for your question about locating days of the week for
past dates.  Our all-volunteer staff is currently swamped with
questions and cannot undertake to do this research for you.
However, I hope we can help you to get started in researching
this information on your own by pointing you to the following
website:

http://www.juneau.com/home/janice/calendarland/
```

Figure 5–5. (Continued)

```
This site has the most extensive collection of calendars on
the Internet, including calendars for the past as well as for the
future.  This is probably the very best place on the Internet
for you to find what you're looking for.

I hope this information is helpful to you.  Good luck in
your research, and thanks for asking the IPL!

> Location: Hilton, NY  USA ... [19 lines quoted]
```

3: Set STATUS to ANSWERED Sat, 09 Aug 1997 17:19:56
    by Lorri Mon (lmon@si.umich.edu)

4: CHANGE SUBJECT to "SCI: Days of the week for past dates" from "IPL Reference Question" Sat, 09 Aug 1997 17:20:33
    by Lorri Mon (lmon@si.umich.edu)

5: TRANSFER to "General Reference Questions TBA" from "Incoming Articles from Mail and HTTP" Sat, 09 Aug 1997 17:20:33
    by Lorri Mon (lmon@si.umich.edu)

Return to Archive File | Category Archive | Top Level Archive | view the User Manual

to dissuade persons wanting to submit questions, but we hoped for the best. At the very least we estimated that the questions we would receive would be "better" ones, so that the entire process would be improved for everyone in the end. I think we were right.

Despite these improvements, there are still some factors that serve as barriers to the question-asking process.

Typing. In e-mail reference, patrons need to be able to type, or at least be able to hunt and peck well enough to enter several lines of text describing their question. We've observed that sometimes an e-mail question is so brief that it is fairly obvious that the user "hasn't gotten into" the subject. We also have received questions consisting only of two or three keywords, which suggested that those users thought they were querying a Web search engine, rather than posing a question to another person via e-mail. (We've since annotated that field on the form to read

"A human being will read your question.") On the other hand, occasionally patrons will give us plenty of wonderful information about their question and their information search, above and beyond what we've asked for.

Language. Not all IPL users speak English; in fact, according to our general IPL Web use statistics, a fair number visit us from countries where English is not the official or primary language. We see that most foreign users will manage to include enough English words in their query that we can at least guess what they are trying to find. We have composed a few answers in Spanish for Mexican patrons, but for most of these users, we cannot respond in their language. (Thai and Malay are good examples, as we receive a measurable number of questions from Thailand and Malaysia.) In these cases we avoid creative and complicated English words in favor of simpler ones, and we also use short sentences in our replies.

Many foreign users ask questions that could be readily answered in a standard United States public library using a garden variety of sources. If the patron were North American it would be easy enough to recommend that he or she visit the local library and ask for a specific source, but when it comes to our foreign users we often are unsure of how readily available, or easy to use, libraries are in any given country. Often these foreign users are students, so one can assume that they have some resources available at school. We wonder about the size and scope of these collections, however, to say nothing of how up-to-date they may be. It's getting easier to send answers in the form of Web sites to foreign IPL patrons, because the Internet is growing so rapidly and answers are more readily available than they once were.

Volume. We receive too many questions at the IPL to answer them all every day. Since about late 1995, after the IPL had been in operation for about eight or nine months, we have never received fewer than 12 questions per day, and we have reached peaks of 50 to 60 questions per day during end-of-semester periods at schools.

As mentioned earlier, every patron who submits a question gets some sort of response—preferably an answer but possibly a "rejection note" explaining that we can't answer the question that day due to volume—as soon as possible. It's really difficult to reject questions (even though it would be even more difficult and painful to try to answer everything, every day!). Most libraries don't have the luxury of turning down questions once they've been asked (though some close the reference desk during certain hours the library is open, so possible questions are never asked in the first place), and we're in the very uncomfortable position of returning a patron's question with the suggestion that they resubmit the question the next day, or consult with a librarian closer to them at their public library or school or workplace. I've worried about unwittingly reinforcing the stereotypical image of the dismissive librarian through our practice of question rejection, though in our form reject response we've taken great pains to be respectful and polite as we explain why we are returning the question unanswered and suggest places where the patron can go for help.

There are also questions that require resources beyond our capabilities, such as requests for extensive data or business analysis or historical research. These questions would require extensive research or sophisticated or costly databases or sources to answer fully. In the beginning of the IPL's operations, we categorized these types of questions as "out of scope" and rejected them, suggesting to patrons that they needed to conduct research on their own, perhaps with the help of an in-person librarian. In November 1997, we stopped using this standard response for the in-depth research questions, and started accepting them as "sources questions," using an acceptance message that indicated that we could only provide some starting points and not complete answers. We still use the out-of-scope message for patrons who ask particularly complicated questions that would be more appropriately directed to legal, medical, religious, or psychiatric professionals.

Timelapse. It would be wonderful if everything were in real-time, but alas, operators are not continuously standing by at the IPL waiting to receive and answer questions, although if the administrator can dispense with a simple or fun question quickly enough, it certainly can happen that the question will be read and answered within minutes of its receipt.

Our intake form includes a field in which patrons indicate a date when the information will no longer be useful to them. We receive many questions that request an answer immediately, often that very day. We made adjustments to our form and Web documentation to inform patrons of the time limitations on our service: that librarians volunteer their time at the IPL, and that answering questions most often is not an instant process.

Age. Children often can't type very efficiently, and they probably won't have the patience to ramble on and on in a form interaction describing the seven facets of their reference question (though they *will* sit for hours on an Internet chat line . . .). We receive many questions from schoolchildren where it's readily apparent to us that they've copied their assignments verbatim into the question box on our form. Children can't, or won't, parse these assignments into pieces small enough to handle manageable library research without help. As a result, it often appears that they are asking "do my assignment for me," when what they really need are starters and prodding to ask more questions themselves. It's often difficult for a remote librarian to discern what direction or focus the child's paper or project will take, or exactly what the child's teacher hoped that the student would gain from the experience. Children, like many adults, often wait until the last minute to think about or prepare for an assignment, which makes it almost impossible to engage in an e-mail dialogue about their question. And, like anyone doing research in a library, they want the pain to be over with as quickly as possible.

IMPORTANT CHARACTERISTICS OF ANY REFERENCE OPERATION

High-quality virtual reference is built on the same characteristics that typify high-quality reference service in person or by phone.

Be nice. Does it really need to be stated? The e-mail reference process is a new thing for everyone, and the range of patron electronic sophistication runs the gamut from experienced folks who've been on the Web since 1993, to the novices who picked up their WebTV control panel at Best Buy last night to see what all the fuss is about the Internet. People deserve the benefit of the doubt, if they are adventurous enough to submit a personally relevant question into the (possible) Internet void, it's your responsibility to look after that question and make their experience worth it. Librarians who answer questions must be able to phrase their responses thoughtfully with sensitivity and humor that comes across in e-mail as closely as it would in person.

Address the patron by name. Occasionally e-mail questions come into the IPL inbox without any identification except for an e-mail username (for example, HiHoPop6@aol.com), but we encourage patrons to identify themselves at least with a first name. Most are happy to oblige. In return, I believe that writing "Dear Jennifer" or "Hi Doug" at the beginning of a reply communicates that the librarian recognizes that the recipient of the message is a library patron—someone whom we are helping—rather than simply the recipient of a URL or a short answer. The salutation also communicates that the person composing the response, the librarian, is a person too, not an automaton or a database of pre-composed answers (like the computer in *Desk Set*). We believe it's important for the patron asking the question to know that there will be a real person on the other end, one with a sincere interest in finding just the answer the patron wants.

Explain things (you might have to go out of your way to do it). Your patron may not know what an index is for, or what an OPAC does (or what's in it), or what the proper process is to try to obtain an item that's not there on the shelf, or that a RealAudio download is necessary to hear a broadcast from the National Public Radio Web site that precisely answers his or her question?

Yes, it takes much longer to compose a response that includes extra information that was not directly asked for (for example, a sentence explaining what the *Encyclopedia of Associations* is, or your thought process behind a certain research path you chose that may not be readily apparent). But in the long run the patron will expect and appreciate the time you took, and will learn from that experience, and be better prepared to ask a "good" question next time.

In face-to-face reference interactions, we think nothing of explaining to patrons what it is that we are looking for as we search an online database, or what's on the section of the reference shelf that we are heading for, as we walk over there with them in tow. Those explanations, which include the patron in the process of answering his or her question, are a de facto part of a good reference encounter. E-mail reference should also contain those qualities.

Try to determine from the question posed what he or she already knows, or ask the patron via a short preliminary response. Sometimes it helps to read the question three or four times. In e-mail, it also helps to be liberal with an interpretation; for example, when volunteer Sue Dirani answered a question requesting a book on Nova Scotia, she sent back several book citations and Web site reviews, covering history, tourism, and local city information, assuring him that if he needed further help he should feel free to write back.

Remember, a satisfactory answer in an e-mail reference venue should consist of much more than just a list of Web sites or article citations. With so many new tools, it's often necessary to explain to Internet patrons how to use the resources we direct them to, just as we would in person. At the IPL we also make a regular habit of pointing out the resources that might be available at their local libraries. Often the books that librarians keep behind the reference desk are just the things the patron needs to know about! Happily, patrons often provide us with the positive feedback we need to get—some of our patrons show their appreciation by sending thank-you notes.

WILLINGNESS TO RETURN

It's extremely important to acknowledge the possibility that you haven't answered the patron's question fully, clarified adequate starting points, or replied in quite the sense that he or she expected, particularly in the virtual reference process. There's no opportunity for instant verification, since you can't see any light of recognition or a confused or frustrated look on the patron's face. Consequently, you must end the e-mail answer with as open-ended a closing as you can manage, and assure the patron that while e-mail correspondence concerning a reference transaction may run in fits and starts due to time gaps and schedules and other behind-the-scenes activity, the reference transaction isn't over until the patron is happy. This helps the patron feel comfortable sending back a follow-up question or other response. At the IPL, our standard closing is usually along the lines of "I hope this information helped you. Please feel free to write again if you need more help or have another question. Thanks for asking the IPL!" If an answer is long-winded (as many can become) or potentially confusing, it's a good idea to admit that fact, and to specifically invite another follow-up question from the patron—perhaps write something like "I hope this information is helpful. If it's not quite what you're looking for, we're very willing to make another try. Please write again if you need more help." We'd like to acknowledge the possible gaps in our understanding of the question, while standing by the work that we've already done.

The trouble with such caretaking in replies is that composing answers takes a long time. While an in-person reference interaction could take ten minutes, the same description of sources and pointers could take 20 minutes to prepare in e-mail—even if you know just the source the patron needs and don't have to search for it on the Web! I have to admit that my typing skills improved immeasurably in the time I worked for the IPL; it was imperative to be able to polish off questions as efficiently as possible, and to save time for the really important parts—finding good sources and then explaining them clearly to patrons. Cutting and pasting relevant portions of text from Web sites, and adding URLs really helps save time too.

STAFF CONCERNS

Somehow, the strains of answering reference questions via e-mail really show when the person answering the question feels pushed into it, or if he or she has concerns other than the question and patron at hand, for example, extra workload, uncertainty about e-mail, concern about managerial moves. Presumably, any remote reference service is started to provide better service to patrons. I advise anyone starting a remote reference service to clarify the reasons for the service to go forward, and to ensure staff buy-in. As with any new project, when workers feel that their contributions and opinions are valued, they are much more likely to react positively to the unknown.

At the IPL, our reference staff consists of a mix of library students from the School of Information and librarian volunteers from other libraries across the Internet (most are from the United States and Canada). Since library students receive course credit for their work at the IPL, we require that they answer a set number of questions per week or term; the actual number varies from term to term as we tried to find the perfect balance between project work in the class (which was also a requirement) and contributions to the daily operation of the library.

I often wished that there were better incentives than grades to entice students to answer questions and to consider the patron's needs above their own wish to earn an A and/or to simply complete the class. The most satisfactory answers were provided by students who enjoyed the "hunt" and were intellectually stimulated by the newness of e-mail communication with people they didn't know, who enjoyed interviewing patrons in non-real-time. These natural reference librarians came to light very quickly in each class.

Students who were disinterested in the process of reference as an art, or who were perhaps not as emotionally tied to the Internet Public Library were more apt to perform the absolute bare minimum required to answer a question—they almost never engaged in any further questioning of the patron, were more likely to take a question at face value and ignore any language nuances or possible pitfalls, and were more likely to send faulty URLs or assume the patron understood how to navigate the Web pages recommended.

Admittedly, the IPL as a classroom is very different from any library that undertakes remote reference as part of its business, but it's just as important for any manager or planner to recognize and address the overriding concerns of his or her workers. Are they worried about how searching the Web or typing out answers will cut into their already tight working hours? Are they concerned that their answers will be read and judged by a supervisor after they've been sent? Are they uncomfortable sending off answers to a patron who may or may not reply or acknowledge their work?

One common complaint I encountered from SI students was that the questions I was accepting were "too hard." Gosh, I only passed on the questions that people asked us—it was never as though I was saving anything up for a six-month-long slew of difficult questions. But I tried to recognize that the students were new at reference sources and strategies. One week I experimented by accepting a set of questions of varying levels of difficulty, and posting to each QRC item a list of possible places for an answer, in the hopes that students would take the hint and check the sources for the actual answer, then compose a complete answer for the patron. It didn't seem to work, though—the difficult questions, for the most part, remained unclaimed or my suggested sources appeared to have been completely ignored. I could at least tell myself that I had them mostly answered by the time I e-mailed the responses.

Constant communication with staff is probably the key to a smooth operation. At the IPL, I often worked at question administration very late into the night, usually well past midnight (try and guess the origins of the IPL reference slogan, "The Day Begins at Midnight"). I liked working late because I have natural night-owl habits, but it also allowed me to tally up IPL statistics for a solid day in one fell swoop, rather than piecing together short numbers from throughout the day. Unfortunately, working at night meant that I wasn't always available during the day when students milled around between classes at SI. Furthermore the IPL offices were not in the same building as where the IPL classes were held.

Once in awhile, however, late at night, I'd notice that a few other IPL staff members were also online (the School of Information has a UNIX system which allows you to see who's logged in). Even better, as I worked accepting questions, those questions would be claimed, possibly even answered, within minutes. I could then send short e-mail notes to the students to say hello and to thank them for jumping in so quickly. Students realized that by working "around me" they'd have first dibs on the pool of questions, but I also felt that by interacting with QRC at the same time, it was almost as though we were working in the same room.

I believe that for staff who may not be as comfortable in a virtual environment, some extra contact with their supervisors just to touch base on the new projects may go a long way toward making them more confident in their searching skills and written or e-mailed reference replies.

FINAL THOUGHTS

Reference service on the Internet requires many of the same qualities as traditional reference: accuracy, promptness, courtesy, an understanding of the information need. And while there may be a disadvantage in not having a face-to-face encounter, there are many advantages to this new medium. The person who is best qualified can answer the question. The question can wait in a queue until there is some breathing room. The reference librarian has time to reflect if necessary. And the greatest advantage—many more people can be helped by using electronic reference services.

Yes—this new medium does require adapting skills and some new considerations. But those of us at the IPL who have worked in a virtual environment are convinced that it pays to invest the time and energy.

Chapter 6

Handling Money Matters

Joseph Janes

When I give presentations about the IPL to library groups or classes or at conferences, or when I just talk about it with people, the conversation usually begins with all the things we've done, and how great a site it is, what a wonderful service we provide, and how terrific it is that librarians did all this. After a few minutes, almost invariably, someone asks, "So who pays for all this?" (If we had a dollar for every time we've been asked that, we'd have a very different answer!) That's an interesting question, and one that goes very much to the heart of the nature of the IPL's work, and how it differs from other libraries. It also, though, indicates that people are not only interested in the IPL's funding situation, but also more generally in funding for library-related activities in a networked environment. When I tell this part of our story, people get quiet, mad, or both.

In this chapter, we want to tell this fascinating and frustrating part of the story. It's probably clear from reading this book that everyone involved in the IPL has learned a great deal about a great many things. It is this area—funding and support—where our most painful and perhaps most valuable lessons have come. We'll look first at a bit of financial background information, followed by several examples of approaches or ideas or projects we have considered or tried to make the IPL economically self-sustaining. After that follows some overall discussion of what has happened so far and why and what applicability it might have for other libraries and organizations.

BACKGROUND

So why does the IPL need money in the first place? It is true that in many cases we take advantage of the great students at the University of Michigan (and elsewhere), who actually pay tuition to work in the reference service. It is also true that we need little or no money for acquisitions (in the classical sense of the term): we don't buy, license, or rent any of our materials. All the items in our collections are either things that we built or that are freely available Web resources. Furthermore, the School of Information has been generous in its continuing support of the IPL, offering not only office space, heat and light, access to the university's library and computing infrastructure, some equipment, and clerical support, but also direct financial support from grants from the W. K. Kellogg Foundation. They also have been most helpful in many of the attempts discussed below to generate other sources of revenue.

And yet, the IPL is an expensive proposition. Student work is enormously valuable, and the IPL has always been an educational enterprise, but such an enterprise requires a core of full-time, professional staff to provide continuity and institutional memory as well as guidance, advice, support, policy making, and other administrative duties (fund-raising, for example). In general, our full-time professional staff (all recent graduates from Michigan who have been involved with the IPL for some time) have taken on coordination and administrative responsibilities in collections, reference, services to young people, public relations, fund-raising, and technology management. Our full-time staff has ranged from 1.5 to 6 FTEs, not including the director (half of an appointment which also included teaching within the school). We also have modest ongoing operating expenses for telephone, postage, duplication, travel, equipment, software, books and magazines, part-time clerical staff, t-shirts (everybody who works with us gets one!), and so on. At least 75 percent of our budget is in staff, and in many cases it has exceeded even this fairly high proportion.

The skills we are looking for do not, as a rule, come cheaply. The IPL doesn't employ shelvers or pages; instead we need people who can program in Perl and design Web pages using Photoshop and write proposals on the cutting edge of libraries, computing, network technology, and education. As an organization, we have been blessed with high-quality people who have been willing to be underpaid (often severely) for the opportunity to work in a fairly cool environment.

So while the school has been very good to us, more has always been needed. Understand, as you read the rest of this account, that we have always been a hand-to-mouth, marginally funded entity, and have never had more than a nine-month horizon to when the money would visibly run out. Our history is one of last-minute transfusions based on people thinking we're really cool and can't possibly go under. Three years of that can be extremely trying, but also more than a little instructive.

THE CURRENT SITUATION

As of summer of 1998, the IPL has 1.5 FTE professional employees and a cadre of about 8 students participating in significant ways, including administrative and supervisory roles, especially in reference and youth services. The professionals include 1.0 FTE in collections (with other duties in technology, teaching, and administration), 0.5 in technology (with other duties in fund-raising). Our reference service has alternately been a staff and student-run position. The director's salary is handled centrally through the School of Information and so does not appear on the IPL budgets. Excepting that amount, the IPL's total budget for this academic year is not much more than $100,000.

FUNDING APPROACHES IN A VIRTUAL LIBRARY WORLD

In this section, I discuss some of the ideas we've had for ways to generate revenue; some we've actively tried, others have just been good ideas that we haven't been able to pursue due to lack of human or financial resources. In the spring of 1996, the Andrew W. Mellon Foundation granted us $200,000 to develop several projects aimed at ensuring the long-term viability of the IPL by giving it a steady and sustainable revenue stream. Many of the projects described below were funded by that grant. Projects are described in no particular order.

Advertising

Advertising is a common method of generating revenue in the Internet world. A great many high-quality sites (and many which aren't so hot) are supported by advertising revenue, and they sell space on their Web pages for banners at the top or bottom of their pages.

These advertisements have become increasingly sophisticated, as have the advertisers' methods of determining how many people are reading them, and of doing anything about it. One hears a great deal about "impressions" (we use the term "visits"), which is simply the number of people who view a page and, presumably, its advertising message. This figure is roughly equivalent to the circulation of a newspaper or magazine or the rating of a television program. However, the Internet allows a more advanced method of knowing how many people are doing something as a result of seeing advertising. The "click-through" rate, the proportion of people who click on an advertising banner to go through to the advertiser's site, is a much better way of measuring the impact of an ad, and in fact many ad contracts now are based on click-throughs rather than impressions.

We've been through several iterations of the ad thing. In the early days, most people in the project (but not everybody) felt it was inappropriate for us to take advertising, that we would appear to be selling out, and besides other libraries wouldn't do it. That's not strictly true, of course—other libraries accept donations from corporations to name a room, endow a collection, or sponsor a special program—but advertising per se doesn't really come up much in the day-to-day library world. So we went the way of looking for "sponsors." That effort was hampered by a couple of factors: we didn't really know what we were doing in this realm, and our traffic wasn't enough to generate substantial income to merit the difficulty (technological and political) of taking advertising.

Over the years, we've probably all accepted the reality that this is how money is generated on the Internet, at least to date, and we have been actually prepared to take advertising. We've also had some interesting conversations with the university (as a part of the University of Michigan we can accept advertising and several offices do, but we can't advocate a particular product or service), but nobody could really give us a straight or simple answer to "Can we sell ad space on our Web site?"

Should other libraries accept that advertising? I don't know for sure, but I'm inclined to say no. Something about it still makes me uncomfortable, especially for public libraries, which should be receiving the overwhelming measure of their support from their communities. I don't want to appear contradictory here, but my inclination is that if a public or academic library started taking ads, it would be a public relations problem at the least (inside and outside the library). If we found an appropriate advertising partner, we'd probably take the ads and lose some respect in some people's—mainly other librarians'—eyes, although many librarians have told me they thought we should go for it, especially if could help us survive and improve. Since we do not have a community or institution to support us, we are very open to going the way of the Net, and accepting advertising.

Partnerships with Corporations

Rather than pursue advertising, we researched corporations that seemed good candidates for sponsoring portions of the library. We developed a press kit, which was mailed to several companies, and followed up with phone calls to each. We met with representatives of the Kellogg Corporation and Borders Books, but little progress was made, and we became discouraged with what for all intents and purposes was really a "cold call" approach. (For those who have never done it, this is extremely difficult. Trust us.)

Then we switched tacks. Inspired by an article in the *Harvard Business Review*,[1] instead of asking corporations to sponsor portions of the IPL, we floated the idea of a marketing alliance that provides mutual benefit for the company and the IPL. In 1997 we made contact with our first corporation, America Online (AOL). At a subsequent phone meeting between the director of the IPL, the dean of the University of Michigan School of Information (SI), and a vice president of marketing at AOL, we were given indication that AOL was interested in further discussing the idea of some sort of alliance with the IPL. However, AOL's interest was purely in the corporate philanthropy vein, an enterprise they intended to launch in their 1997–1998 fiscal year, not as a marketing alliance. This deferred discussion until late summer 1997; subsequent personnel changes at AOL complicated matters further. Unfortunately, later discussions went nowhere, even though we had a solid idea and proposal, and an introduction to a senior executive at AOL who seemed genuinely interested in helping us. We just were speaking very different languages.

Separately, Infonautics, which provides premium online content for consumers, particularly through its flagship Electric Library reference service, approached us and declared interest in a partnership. They flew two IPL staff members to their corporate headquarters to begin negotiations. Their final offer called for a search bar on the IPL site to provide access to both IPL and Electric Library materials, banner advertising on the IPL site, and licensing of IPL content as participation in a new proprietary effort for the K–12 market. They were unable to provide funding guarantees beyond the third quarter of 1997. This proposal also appeared to be a sincere effort on their part to find a way to support the IPL, but in the end it was not sufficient to justify such a large commitment on our part.

We remain convinced that corporate partners could provide a substantial portion of our revenue. The approach of cold calling corporations for sponsorships or partnerships seems doomed to fail—we have to have personal connections with high-level executives at these companies. Our efforts in this area would be vastly improved if we had a staff member with experience in corporate development. Such a person could help our current initiatives and could also test other methods of corporate development that we have not pursued.

Individual Donations or Memberships

Starting in April 1996 the IPL Web site included an area that allows individuals to make donations to the organization. When initially launched, the library home page included a link to this section, and the pages still exist in our "About the Library" section. We received very few (fewer than ten) individual unsolicited contributions. This number might have been increased with greater publicity and stronger focus; however, we believed that attention to larger sources (corporate and foundation support) was more promising.

The model of selling memberships is not without precedent, though. Before about 1875 many libraries in the United States were subscription libraries, funded by individual memberships which gave people the privilege to use and borrow materials. Benjamin Franklin's Library Company in Philadelphia is a notable example. It was only in the twentieth century that the free public library we know today became commonplace, largely due to the philanthropy of Andrew Carnegie. Would membership work for us? Probably not. Why should people pay for it if it's already free?

Fee-Based Research

We researched the feasibility of launching a fee-based extended research service. After reading up on the field, meeting the representatives from the University of Michigan's existing fee-based research service, MITS, and analyzing the competition, we concluded that it is very hard to make a profit in this field, that the market for a low-end, fee-based service is unproven, and that we lack access to the massive amount of capital necessary to launch such a service.

Other libraries would probably face similar problems for two additional reasons. First, there is not yet a secure, trusted method of payment on the Internet. Credit card purchases are now common for things like books, CDs, and airline tickets, but trying to get small amounts of money for, say, viewing an individual page would be very difficult. Second, people (at least in the public library world) are not accustomed to paying for this kind of information. It's different in the corporate world and somewhat different in academe, but many people would rather fumble with search engines or Yahoo or the IPL or the Library of Congress Web site to look for an answer to their question than pay somebody over the Internet to do high-quality research for them. (For that matter, they'd rather ask a friend for help than call their local public library, but we all know that problem.) The "good enough" phenomenon is fairly deeply ingrained and does not bode well for fee-for-service programs in general, let alone those based on the still iffy Internet resource environment.

Services to Other Libraries, Continuing Education, Licensing Our Intellectual Property

The idea of creating an Internet Library Consortium, a federated network of libraries and librarians with which we could share our work, expertise, and lessons was exciting and promising, but proved much too ambitious. In our market research discussions with librarians, each wanted something different. And the process of developing a consortium took much longer than expected given our lack of resources. Rather than creating a consortium, we pursued its various components separately. Selling our expertise (through licensing our intellectual property, through providing continuing education and training, and through consulting) is, however, still a good idea.

LICENSING OUR INTELLECTUAL PROPERTY: SOFTWARE AND COLLECTIONS

Many libraries are interested in using QRC, the custom software we developed and use to help manage our Ask a Question e-mail reference service. We've had many offers to test our library groupware product at no charge; to date the software is used at Oakland University and the West Bloomfield Public Library and we have received unsolicited inquiries from several other libraries. The Dow Chemical corporate library purchased a software license for $10,000 and they will modify the software to suit their needs.

In early 1997 we received contact from a publisher who was interested in putting portions of the IPL's cataloging records collections on a CD-ROM of freely available texts. We agreed on terms ($2,500 advance, plus 10 percent of gross profit on wholesale), but the publisher elected not to complete the contract due to their financial constraints.

CONTINUING EDUCATION, TRAINING, AND DISSEMINATION

The IPL has conducted three successful summer institutes, welcoming professional librarians from the United States, Spain, Mexico, Kuwait, and Cyprus for two-and-a-half-day workshops on the use and integration of the Internet and networked information resources in reference and collection development activities. These workshops were oversubscribed and well received. In total, this has been among our most productive work, netting us something more than $20,000 over the last two years, and it reinforces the notion that selling our expertise is among our most viable ways to generate revenue.

Our efforts in this area have always been productive and well received. Although labor-intensive, training sessions and writing increase visibility for our work and allows us to share our lessons with our professional colleagues as well as the wider Internet community. It is unlikely that this area alone would generate sufficient revenue to support the rest of the library's work, but it is an important potential continuing source of support.

Grants and Project Work

Though short-term grants do not put us on the road toward economic sustainability, they do put money in our coffers and help pave the way for additional partnerships in the future. The School of Information has been extremely generous to the IPL. In the spring of 1996, they agreed to contribute $150,000 in cash, over a three-year period, for the general support of the library, plus the salary and benefits of the director. In addition, they have continued to provide us with office space, as well as some computer hardware and software.

We also received project-based support from other divisions of the University of Michigan. The Office of Academic Outreach provided $50,000 for two projects on increasing technological and computer literacy and teamwork into the K–12 curriculum.

In addition, we undertook a consulting arrangement with the AskERIC project at Syracuse University as part of their Virtual Reference Desk initiative; we designed and built a searchable database of archives of asked and answered questions from a number of virtual reference services (including the IPL).

Our relationship with Michigan—and SI in particular—has been very helpful. We would not exist today were it not for these grants. But such relationships tend not to support the whole library, and they do not last forever. They can be important sources of income in the short term but they are not a viable path toward long-term economic stability.

Over the years, we have explored a great many other potential sources of foundation or philanthropic funding. Some foundations are interested in funding public libraries, but since we really aren't a public library in a legal sense, we don't qualify. Our use of technology is innovative and groundbreaking, but not original in the sense of developing new technologies, so technology funding isn't available. Further, many foundations will not provide general operating support. We have wondered, from time to time, whether it would be easier to get support to *start* the IPL over again than to maintain or grow it from its current excellent if unstable position.

Helping Children, Parents, and Teachers Get the Most from the Net with a Newsletter

We launched *WebINK: Internet Newsletter for Kids* in July 1996 (see Chapter 4). *WebINK* was a bimonthly 12-page newsletter available to students, their parents, teachers, and school media centers for $19.95 per year. We received orders for several hundred subscriptions, and a very positive reaction from the school library and educational communities.

WebINK's success was quite good for a start-up publication, but the enterprise needed many more resources to be viable economically. We pursued ways of partnering strategically with publishers or organizations (Time-Warner, the American Library Association, Classroom Connect, Songline Studios) to handle marketing and distribution of the publication, but without success.

Our original forecast was to be self-sustaining in the second year; most publications typically require three years. The industry average for subscription returns based on advertising and sample issues is 2 percent; *WebINK* averaged 5 to 6 percent. It is clear that a profitable market exists for a product like *WebINK*, which offered educational and curricular resources tied to the Internet. With more advertising resources and a sharper earlier focus on marketing, a response rate such as that generated by an advertisement in the Winter 1997 issue of *School Library Journal* (12 percent) would have made a significant difference. Unfortunately, we had to suspend publication after the first year, due to a lack of resources.

Going Strong despite the Odds

It is particularly hard to make money providing Internet content. Though a good number of hardware and software companies are making money selling Internet products (for example, Cisco Systems), Internet companies that provide content are not, by and large, profitable. An exception is Yahoo, which, for the last year or so, has hovered around the break-even point. Among the high-profit Web sites that have scaled back drastically or closed their doors entirely are the Utne Lens, Web Review, the Spot, Out.com, and Stim.

A March 1997 study from the Magazine Publishers of America (MPA) conducted by Ernst & Young titled "The Business of Online Publishing," found that fewer than 20 percent of survey respondents (47 MPA members that produce 287 traditional print publications and 17 online-only brand magazines) are making a profit online. "Those few companies already profiting from online activities are doing so with the digital extensions of their print magazines and not from start-up, on-line only publications."[2]

William Bass, Senior Analyst of Media and Technology Strategies at Forrester Research, states, "Sites that say they're profitable—I don't buy it. We think most sites are covering maybe 20 percent of their costs."[3] Adam Schoenfeld, an analyst at Jupiter Communications, states, "Just like 80 out of every 100 new magazines fold, I wouldn't be surprised if a similar percentage of new Web sites go under."[4] The fact that the IPL still exists, after over three years on this Web, is testimony to the idea that we must be doing something right.

Getting Outside Funding for Your Library's Web Site

We have sampled a variety of methods of revenue generation and have learned a lot about what it takes to achieve economic sustainability.

ECONOMIC SUSTAINABILITY OUTLOOK FOR INTERNET-BASED NONPROFITS

- *Good publicity and reputation only go so far.* The IPL has had much good publicity and a large patron base. These factors gave us access to organizations like AOL and Infonautics, but we found it hard to translate this goodwill into financial capital.
- *It takes a lot of money to develop and maintain high-quality Internet services.* The dynamism and lack of central authority that make the Web an exciting and creative place also mean that Web resources move and change and grow and die often and unpredictably. Therefore, any attempt to organize them is time- and resource-consuming.
- *A good way to acquire start-up capital is to partner with corporations.* Such relationships are a win-win situation, once the right corporate partners have been selected and convinced.
- *The tighter the focus the better.* We spread ourselves too thin with too many enterprises, serving too big (and too varied) an audience.

ECONOMIC SUSTAINABILITY OUTLOOK FOR LIBRARIES IN THE INFORMATION AGE

The IPL is unique among libraries in that it has no tax base, the traditional economic model that serves public libraries in North America. While a good number of our difficulties stem from our uniqueness, we have learned the following lessons that will be of interest to other libraries:

- *Selling expertise to companies and other librarians is a good way to make money.* Our pioneering efforts in the Internet environment have positioned us well to offer our expertise to others (for example, SI workshops, software license sold to Dow Chemical library, this book).
- *A library Web site should have a well-defined mission and focus.* Traditional libraries serve many functions (for ex-

ample, they provide a safe space, offer instruction in the use of information, maintain collections, answer reference questions). Any attempt to translate these functions into the networked environment should identify and make clear what it is meant to achieve and why.

- *The public does not understand the cost of information and reference service.* This is not a news flash, but is particularly relevant in the Internet environment, where consumers, who are already paying the phone company and their Internet service provider, are reluctant to pay for Internet content.

- *People expect the same things from libraries on the Internet that they expect in person.* Our contact with our patrons leads us to believe that people expect from us what they expect from a traditional library: current books in electronic form, literary criticism, indexes, back issues of periodicals, personalized assistance, and relatively prompt service.

The Importance of the Right Organizational Team

- *Business experience is essential.* The entire IPL staff that was hired at the onset of the grant (except for our computer scientist) were librarians—dedicated and extremely well-qualified. But none of the staff has significant work experience outside of libraries or academia. If we had to do it over again, we would have at least one staff member with proven business experience. At the outset, we felt that we could learn skills in marketing, management, development, and strategic planning on the job, but that assumption proved costly. We came in with considerable intangible capital and goodwill—in terms of our use, our publicity, and the dedication of the staff—but we were not able to transform those resources into dollars, due to our lack of experience.

- *Access to influential people is extremely important.* Having friends in high places—who have access to friends in high places—is very helpful.

IN RETROSPECT

We wanted money to keep the library going. Our code phrase for this was "middle money": money we could use for the core operations of the library (building and maintaining collections, reference, collections for kids), including salaries and general operating income. In practice, that sort of money is extremely difficult to come by, especially from foundations and grants— the sources we were pursuing. We had many offers and ideas for more project-based funding: the Infonautics endeavor would have been of this sort, but we constantly felt that taking on specific projects would distract us from the core that made us interesting and what we were. We tried in most cases to build "overhead" or middle money into those projects, but that was never easy. We also got sidetracked by many of these opportunities—each of them looked good and sounded interesting, and besides we needed the money, so spending days or weeks pursuing them, talking with people, planning, writing proposals, and so on took substantial energy and a significant toll.

We were chasing the money for a long time. Instead, it might have been more effective to focus on a few things or even one (*WebINK*, perhaps, or QRC licensing) and devote a great deal of time and effort to just that. It might not have made much of a difference, but our strategy of trying everything clearly didn't work. That strategy was born of a feeling that none of these enterprises individually would completely fund us, so we had to make them all successful. That feeling was more than likely correct, but in the end nothing worked because they were all undercapitalized and we lacked experience in vital areas of each.

What about the government? We looked at a variety of federal grant programs, including ones from the National Science Foundation (NSF), NASA, the National Endowment for the

Humanities, and the Department of Education. Again, this was project-based money (the proposal to the NSF for a virtual science fair for home-schooled students still sounds like a winner to me), and our global nature transcends the interest of any particular government—local, state, or even national.

Our global nature, I think, is central to our money travails. Calling ourselves a "public library" simultaneously enabled our work—made it visible and interesting—and doomed it.

The public library metaphor helped enormously in structuring and focusing efforts in building the library and adding to it. It was an attractive idea from the beginning, drawing in people who were intrigued by its admittedly catchy name. The name was immediately intriguing and provocative, and made people want to know more about it, and it was a significant help in early publicity efforts.

But—public libraries are free. Or at least that's what most people think and perceive. They don't stop to think that tax money or public money of some sort supports all the information and people and services found in their local public libraries. We compounded this problem by being a public library—a free entity—on the Internet, and we all know that most information on the Net is free. So we were doubly free and thus why did we need money to continue? Once the situation is explained to individuals, they understand, but it's a nontrivial explanation at best.

Perhaps many of us thought that we would become such a successful, valuable, and worthwhile resource that the Internet community would rise to our defense and develop mechanisms to tax themselves to support our work. Who knows—it might happen someday, but it's unlikely. The Internet is not a community. If anything, it's a meeting place, a conversation, a shared set of protocols that enable a great many interesting things to happen. If it evolves into anything more, something resembling a government that collects and disburses money to support good works, it will take quite some time to happen.

In our case, we were (and are) a public library without a community or means of support. If there is an organization, company, or foundation whose mission includes maintaining a free public library for all people on the Internet, we haven't found it yet. The School of Information has supported us as an educational enterprise, but only as such, and the Mellon Foundation was much more interested in not-for-profit organizations and their sustainability in a networked environment than in supporting an Internet library.

It may be that we are simply ahead of our time, that the evolution of public libraries in the networked environment will follow that of public libraries in the real world. First, we had subscription libraries, where people paid annual fees for the use of the collections—and Electric Library, a product of Infonautics, looks a great deal like a subscription library. After some time, communities realized that they wanted all people to have access to information, and so public libraries as we know them today arose, with substantial help from Andrew Carnegie, around a century ago. Perhaps this process must repeat itself, and perhaps the IPL will still be around to take advantage of the outcome.

NOTES

1. Alan R. Andreason. "Profits for Nonprofits: Find a Corporate Partner." *Harvard Business Review* 74, no. 6 (November/December 1996): 47–60.
2. See www.ey.com/tce/ for more information.
3. Keith J. Kelly, "Critics Dispute Online Profit Outlook," *Advertising Age* (November 18, 1996): 10.
4. Seth Schiesel, "Some Media Organizations Pull the Plug on Web Sites," *The New York Times*, 25 March 1997, search.nytimes.com/web/docsroot/library/cyber/week/032597shakeout.html. This is now archived.

Epilogue

Joseph Janes

This seems an appropriate time for a few reflections on where we've been and where we're going, both at the IPL and in the profession at large.

WHY THE IPL HAS SUCCEEDED

I think there are five reasons why the IPL has been such an interesting place and why our work has been so well received.

1. It starts with the *people* we've been blessed to work with: extraordinarily talented people from a wide variety of backgrounds.
2. We have always set very high *standards* for our work, at first because of the kind of people we are and also because the world was watching. And then we kept our standards high because we had a reputation to live up to.
3. The people involved have always been highly *motivated*— at first by deadlines and external pressure, later for innate reasons—simply because they were obsessed with the project.
4. There has always been a spirit of *creativity*, born in equal parts of brains and poverty: we find a way to do things, invent a way, or find someone else who knows more than we do.
5. And finally, and first, was the power of the *idea*. I have

learned that the word "library" carries great power and respect for most people, and our work has succeeded to the extent that we have carried on the great tradition of innovation and service of the librarians who have gone before us. I only hope that the IPL continues to grow and improve.

THE IPL TOMORROW

After three years, several million users, and a lot of hard work, what happens next? I'm often asked about how we might do things differently if we were to do it again or start over. In many ways, the IPL is a very traditional library, in terms of the services it provides, and the ideas that motivate it. To be sure, the environment in which it operates is new and exciting, but there are new frontiers that could be explored. Following are six ideas for the future:

1. **Use new technologies.** Our concern for equality of access to our site means that our pages are quite simple, quick to load, and dominated by text. It also means we don't get a chance to play with new technologies like Java and Shockwave, or explore things like XML. These technologies are important, though, because they form the basis for the technological environment. They also get noticed, and people think they're cool. While I don't think we need lots of animated images and sound files on all our pages, we could try to find ways to investigate and incorporate these new technologies as appropriate without sacrificing access and thus serve as a testbed for a more significant technological development enterprise.

2. **Use metadata.** The concept of metadata has, of course, been around for quite a while, and librarians are familiar with it through cataloging and indexing. In the Internet world, however, it's becoming increasingly important, in simple ways (like using <META> tags to influence search

engine behavior) and in more sophisticated approaches (such as the work of the Dublin Core and Warwick Framework groups). This is clearly an area where librarians should participate and the IPL seems a perfect opportunity for experimentation and testing of potentially useful ideas.

3. **Use licensed and proprietary materials.** At present, the IPL collections only have pointers to freely available Web-based resources. These are of interest and value, but there are so many more and better resources, produced by commercial publishers and available through fee-based licenses. It is intriguing to think about potential arrangements with publishers or vendors or other Web-based services which could combine the best of both worlds, and be of benefit to us and our users.

4. **Scale up our work.** We are a small operation with a grand scope and vision. Unfortunately, we have always been limited by our resources and size. Could the IPL serve more people around the world, answering those 500 reference questions a day, having a million people a day visiting the site and finding the information they want or need? Thinking hard about ways in which we could scale up, distribute, or federate our work would be very interesting indeed.

5. **Support our work more fully.** Obviously, without support, no further ideas can be realized. The School of Information at Michigan has been very good to us, but it is not in their mission to fund a free public library for the world, other than as a limited, educational enterprise for their students. A more entrepreneurial outlook—creating partnerships with other entities that understand what we do and that can be of mutual assistance—would move us toward broad, stable, and sustainable support for the IPL.

6. **Establish a closer connection to the profession and to our users.** This may be the most important idea of all. Reaching out to our colleagues in the library and information professions as well as to our users, and understand-

ing what they find of value in the IPL, how we can be better, and how we can take advantage of their talents and help, can give us the power that makes the Internet so strong—the power of distribution and cooperation.

BEYOND THE BEGINNING: WHAT WE HAVE LEARNED

Now the IPL is beyond its infancy. We have been visited several million times from users in over 130 countries, and answered many thousands of reference questions. We are presently averaging over 20,000 users per day, an average of one about every four seconds, 24 hours a day. Our collections now number over 20,000 items, including nearly 8,000 pointers to online texts, 2,700 reference resources, 2,500 serials, 2,000 newspapers, and 1,200 items for young people. I hope these statistics have been dramatically surpassed by the time you read them.

We have learned several important lessons since the IPL's inception. I'll close with three of the more important ones.

Librarianship Works . . . Almost All the Time

The IPL does many things that almost every other library does, and they're exactly the same and completely different. We answer reference questions, but we can't see people, read their facial expressions or body languages, or even interview them terribly well. We tell stories, but to children we never meet. We select, describe, and organize resources, but we don't catalog. And yet in all these instances, traditional librarianship has guided what we do and how we do it. In fact, when faced with a challenge or problem, we almost always explore approaches from the profession, and more often than not, it's helpful.

There are many times, however, when the traditional approach doesn't work. For example, we have often found that when we send e-mail to people who have asked us reference questions (to follow up or ask for more information), we get no response. Whether it's because they don't check e-mail often, don't care about their question that much, have lost interest, or no longer have e-mail, we don't know. There really isn't an analogy to that in the real world—sometimes patrons do drift away while you're working with them, but it's hard to imagine asking someone a question and then getting no response, and not even knowing if the person is there any more. So what do we do? Answer as best we can? What if the patron truly doesn't care any more? Should we use our scarce resources to answer a question for a patron who has evaporated, as far as we can tell?

Most libraries attempt to build collections that will endure, and of course books and other physical carriers of information will persist. It is, in practice, difficult for us at the IPL to know which "items" in our "collections" are even still there at any given point, whether they have changed, or what's happened to them. Every day when we wake up, our collection is almost certainly different at least in some respect from what it was the day before. This fact certainly makes collection development (and maintenance) a challenge.

The Best Way to Learn It Is to Do It

There is simply no way that any of us could have learned the lessons we have over the years if we hadn't been out there trying. And as we continue to try and do new things, we continue to learn, both from things that work well and from things that don't.

I said over and over in that first class that there was no way for the project to fail. I believed that then and I still do. Regardless of how many people use the IPL, and what they think of it, the only way for the project to fail is if nobody learns from it.

The IPL has always been at its best a vehicle for learning and trying new things. I think of it as a teaching and research library, in the model of teaching and research hospitals, where people come to learn how to heal more effectively and try out new methods of treatment, all the way interacting with real patients and providing a real service. The IPL is much the same; students come to learn about librarianship in the emerging information environment, librarians come to get new perspectives and ideas and continuing education, and thousands of people find the Internet a more hospitable place.

While Technology Is Not the Point, This Case Is Different

Libraries and librarians have become masterful at incorporating new technologies and storage media into their work. Walk into almost any library and you'll see not only books but magazines, newspapers, audio CDs, CD-ROMs, videocassettes, pamphlets, posters, art, and so on, as well as connections to digital resources from commercial vendors and, of course, the Internet. What we have always known is that the medium is less important than the quality of information and that technology can help provide new and better kinds of access to information.

But of course those technologies are not the point. Most libraries have microforms of some flavors, but the incorporation of microfilm or microfiche didn't fundamentally change librarianship. Neither did online resources or CD-ROMs. And, frankly, neither will the simple presence of Internet-based resources. They are simply another set of potential aids in helping people find out more about their world and lives. They do raise some new and fascinating questions about the nature of publishing and authority and the value of the editorial process, but just having access to the Net won't change librarianship or libraries.

Using the Net, though, might. There is a difference to this technology, compared to those that have gone before. The Internet is more than just a new storage medium or search facility. The power of the Net, in librarianship as everywhere else, is its ability to connect—people, organizations, ideas, and information. It *could* permit a sea change and quantum leap forward in the quest to allow people to be more fully informed and aware.

The central problem of librarianship is now and always has been to help get information out of one person's head and into another's. We have been doing this with books and indexes and catalogs—because that's what we've had. When you add the ability to connect directly to people and organizations and communities who know about things and can make the information available, you completely change the paradigm.

You can break it open even wider when you contemplate connecting the *librarians*. Consider the power of thousands of librarians, connected via the Internet, working together on collection development, readers' advisory, reference, storytelling, and all the rest, to serve people in their millions on a daily basis. It staggers the imagination, and places librarianship directly in the middle of a revolution in information provision. The Internet won't be the end of libraries, as many have proclaimed—it could be the beginning of the enshrinement of librarianship and what it stands for as one of the most important, valuable, and respected professions.

Index